# Famous Wisconsin Authors

## James P. Roberts

**Badger Books Inc.**
**Oregon, WI**

Badger Books Inc.
P.O. Box 192
Oregon, WI 53575
Toll-free phone: (800) 928-2372
Fax: (608) 835-3638
Email: books@badgerbooks.com
Web site: www.badgerbooks.com

# CONTENTS

# INTRODUCTION

Welcome to *Famous Wisconsin Authors*. This book began as a series of essays on historic Wisconsin writers in 1998 as part of the state of Wisconsin's sesquicentennial celebration. The essays were published in the magazine *Badger Books Quarterly*: four essays per year (with one interruption) from 1998 until the spring 2001 issue when the publisher decided to fold the magazine. This same publisher has produced the book you now hold in your hands.

It was suggested that these essays be put together, along with a few additional subjects, with a view toward possible book publication. When the go-ahead was given in late July 2001, I settled down into a long haul of serious reading. I read an average of 2,000 pages weekly from mid-August to the end of October. I read all the books listed in the selected reading section at the end of each essay.

I could not have done any kind of justice to this book without the valuable help of several research tools, the most obvious being the Internet with its thousands of Web sites devoted to Wisconsin literature. Most of the authors you see within these pages can be found on the Internet, and several have their own societies of devoted fans. Also valuable were the following books: *The Journey Home: The Literature of Wisconsin Through Four Centuries*, edited by Jim Stephens and published in 1989 by North Country Press of Madison, Wisconsin. Also, *Wisconsin Writers and Writing* by August Derleth, published in 1998 by Hawk & Whippoorwill Press of Sauk City, Wisconsin, and Shelburne, Ontario. A final acknowledgment goes to *Wisconsin Authors and Their Books, 1836-1975*, published by the Wisconsin Department of Public Instruction in 1976. Although I quibble with (actually, I cringe at) that book's listing some of the authors listed in that book as "Wisconsin" authors (Carl Sandburg? Eudora Welty? Joyce Carol Oates?) it, nevertheless, is a fine research tool, and an updated edition is long overdue.

I also used several other fine anthologies of Wisconsin literature to point out the path, but I chose which places on the path to stop and linger. I also established some criteria to judge whether or not a certain person was a "Wisconsin" writer. As is usually the case, the selections were subject to some flexibility, but all the authors included had to be one of the following: 1) Born in Wisconsin and lived a significant portion of their lives within the state; 2) Begun their writing careers while living in Wisconsin and at least one of their works, more usually a significant portion of their total writings, had to have been set in Wisconsin.

Quite often, a famous writer was born in another state or country and came to Madison to attend the University of Wisconsin, stayed for college and then moved on. With only one or two exceptions, these writers are not included. Those that are in *Famous Wisconsin Authors* are known to have done some writing while at the university, usually with a Wisconsin setting.

One excellent modern-day writer in particular is regrettably excluded. She is Margaret George, born in Tennessee and now living in Madison. Margaret George writes what has been called "epic historical fiction," though she prefers to consider them "biographies of famous people." In this area, she is similar to Frederich Prokosch, another Madison writer whose best known works are *The Asiatics, The Skies of Europe* and *Age of Thunder*. Margaret George spent part of her childhood in Israel where her father was stationed before returning to the U.S. She majored in biology and English literature in college and later worked as a science writer for the National Cancer Institute.

Margaret George's first book was *The Autobiography of Henry VIII,* published in 1986 to much critical acclaim. Her "fictional" account of the life of the great English king presented a portrait different from what was commonly known. She returned to the British Isles six years later with *Mary, Queen of Scotland and the Isles,* yet another, more sympathetic look at the embattled and doomed queen. What was already becoming evident with Margaret George's books was the sheer amount of research involved that to some pundits also accounted for the thickness of her books. Nevertheless, one does get drawn into the grandeur and epic scope of the historical dramas being played out within their pages. *The Memoirs of Cleopatra*, published in 1997, is the result of a lifelong interest Margaret George had in the Egyptian queen going back to 1956 when she did a report on Cleopatra as a school project. *The Memoirs* was made into a television mini-series by Hallmark in 1998. A new book, *Mary, Called Magdalene,* is to be published in the summer of 2002.

I regret that this book isn't longer, for there are other fine Wisconsin writers who must also be acknowledged: Laura Ingalls Wilder, Mark Schorer, Edward Harris Heth, Margaret Benbow, Mel Ellis, Justin Isherwood, Herbert Kubly, Sara Rath, Dennis Trudell and many more. It has been a great pleasure to acquaint myself with the plentiful literature that Wisconsin has produced, both yesterday and today. And reading these authors has produced several wonderful stories as well. Did you know that Edna Ferber once wrote a baseball story? That Mountain Wolf Woman's daughter, White Hawk, moved to Waterloo, Iowa, where the local minor league baseball team at that time was known as the White Hawks? That a certain road in western Wisconsin mentioned in the latest Stephen King/Peter Straub novel really exists? Such is the fare of *Famous Wisconsin Authors.* Read on and enjoy.

**— James P. Roberts**

# ZONA GALE

If you travel through Wisconsin on Interstate 90-94, either heading north to Minneapolis or south to Chicago, you approach an exit sign for Portage.

The Highway 51 exit turns into MacFarland Road through the center of town, and if you stay with MacFarland Road you will come to the banks of the Wisconsin River just beyond the intersection with Edgewater Street. Turning to the right, you will see a lovely house with a columned entranceway. In the back of the house is a wide yard that ends at the edge of the river. The scene radiates a sense of calm and easy living. It's the house where Zona Gale lived, and you have come to "Friendship Village."

Portage is aptly named. Nearby is the Fox River, and the French trappers and voyageurs used to carry — *portage* — their canoes and goods across the short distance between the Wisconsin and Fox rivers and paddle on to Green Bay or Prairie du Chien, to sell their winter's catch. It was in Portage that, on August 26, 1874, Zona Gale was born, the only child of Charles Gale and Eliza Beers Gale.

Gale once said: "I inherited predominant elements of character from both parents. From my mother imagination and initiative, from my father reflective and meditative tendencies; from both, power of concentration and whatever of kindness and a socialized nature I have carried on."

Her childhood was markedly serene and uncomplicated, although the Gales moved to Minneapolis when Zona was 4 and she later fell ill with diphtheria, which left her with a fragile, delicate constitution all her life. The Minneapolis sojourn was short-lived and the Gales were back in Portage by the time Zona was 8.

Gale began writing early and was busily sending her stories out to magazines. "The postman's habit was to open the front door and toss mail into the hall. The heavy manuscripts fell with an unmistakable sound; and often, even when I was upstairs, I could count them as they dropped, and knew just how many of my stories had come back."

Gale attended the University of Wisconsin from 1891 to 1895, although she didn't get her master's degree until 1899. While at the university, she got interested in journalism. She moved to Milwaukee in 1895 because she "felt there wasn't anything in Portage that could be written about." For weeks she haunted the office of the editor of the *Milwaukee Evening Wisconsin* asking for work.

Finally, Gale was given an assignment covering a flower show.

Gale lived in Milwaukee from 1895 to 1901. One of her earliest literary influences was Walter Pater; she believed "in the magic of words, the hypnosis of literary styles." In 1901, Zona went to New York where she found work on the *Evening Journal.* She stayed for less than two years, although she would always return there for the winter months until the final year of her life and, back in Portage, began noticing how it was the everyday commonplace things that she could turn into stories. She avoided unpleasantness in her stories, choosing not to write about cruelty, brutality, sex or violence.

In this experience was born *Friendship Village,* written at the same time as a series of stories about an old couple, Pelleas and Etarre, who find ways to bring about young love. But the first book of Gale's to be published, *Romance Island* (1905), was more of a light fantasy.

It was *Friendship Village,* published in 1908, that led Zona Gale to be called "one of the foremost writers of our time." At the time Gale was in the process of building the house overlooking the Wisconsin River that she would eventually return to after her New York period.

While in New York, Gale got involved in the women's movement. She marched in rallies and wrote articles about the need for women to have rights equal to those of men.

Early in her stay, she had met with Charles Hanson Towne, an editor of various magazines. Gale's involvement with causes crept into her fiction. She wrote a series of

**Zona Gale. Photo courtesy of Wisconsin Historical Society. (WHi-2653)**

books that reflected her positions. *Heart's Kindred* is an anti-war novel; *A Daughter of the Morning* argues for better working conditions for women; one of Gale's short stories, "The Reception Surprise," which argued that blacks should have a social position equal to that of whites, never saw publication. It was rejected time and again by editors who seemed to be fearful of such an explosive issue.

Although *Friendship Village* had won for Gale many admirers, it was her next novel that turned Zona Gale into a household name. *Birth,* the simple and realistic story of an ineffectual man named Marshall Pitt, who marries Barbara Ellsworth out of pity and tries to take over her late father's wallpaper-hanging business, showed a new direction in Gale's writing. She was now portraying things not in a "shining light" but as stark everyday reality. In *Birth,* Barbara

Pitt leaves her husband and infant and disappears for much of the novel. Marshall Pitt himself leaves the young boy, Jeffrey, with neighbors while he departs to seek his fortune in the Alaskan gold fields. The story then shifts focus to the village of Burage as young Jeffrey grows up. After fifteen years, Marshall Pitt returns, only to die in a house fire.

Her next book only confirmed to the public that Gale had indeed changed her direction. *Miss Lulu Bett* was an overnight sensation and many considered it to be Zona's finest work. Published in 1920, *Miss Lulu Bett* won the 1921 Pulitzer Prize after Gale had adapted it into a play.

*Faint Perfume,* published in 1923, continued the run of success. Also in 1923, Gale was appointed to the Board of Regents at the University of Wisconsin. She would continue to serve on the board the rest of her life, despite occasional clashes with university policy.

In 1927, Gale's interest in mysticism, always present though beneath the surface, now deepened with the establishment of a school outside of Portage that espoused the philosophy of the noted Russian mystic G.I. Gurdjieff (for more information on this fascinating Russian mystic see Colin Wilson's *G.I. Gurdjieff: The War Against Sleep.*) This concept of "the world beyond the world we know, and one that we can and must rise to," eventually became a part of Gale's fiction. Her mother's death and experience with Gurdjieff brought a mystical influence to her fiction.

*Preface to A Life,* published in 1926, is one of these — a minor novel imbued with Gale's mysticism to the point of being a distraction from the story itself. It was reviewed lukewarmly, most reviewers tending to ignore the mysticism and focus on her delineation of the characters and the town. The next book was another collection of short stories, *Yellow Gentians and Blue.* The stories were a mixture of bitter tragedy and sweet romance, which was reflected in Gale's choice of the title. In 1928, Gale moved to Knopf as publisher of her next three titles. *Portage, Wisconsin and Other Essays* to Gale was more than just a collection of observances. It also examined a way of life.

*Borgia* was a minor work about a young woman who believes that she is the cause of disaster and tragedy to all around her. But Gale had more important things on her mind. She married William Llywelyn Breese, an industrialist and banker, in 1928. Ever since she was a young girl, she had been attracted to Breese, ten years her senior.

She recounts an episode where Breese pulled the fragile child over the snow in a sled, an event that later was used in a story. Breese's first wife had died, and he had a daughter, Juliette. Gale herself had taken in a young girl whom she named Leslyn, though she did not officially adopt her until after their marriage.

Gale's father died in 1929, at the age of 88, and she wrote a beautiful description of the moment of his passing, which she likened to Tennyson's final moments.

*Bridal Pond,* another collection of short stories, was published in 1930, her third of the three books for Knopf. Here is Zona Gale at her best. The stories are sharp, incisive, insightful and, though still tinged with mysticism, show a sharp sense of irony.

Several minor efforts followed. Gale began using the radio to reach out to the public. Twelve episodes of stories selected from the *Friendship Village* books were broadcast, read by Gale herself. In 1933, *Papa La Fleur* was published by Appleton-Century. Portage itself is named in the novel, and many of the traits of Charles Gale can be seen in *Papa La Fleur.* In the foreword to her next collection, *Old Fashioned Tales* (1933), Gale gives a capsule account of her *raison d'etre* for writing: "One discerns, while being amused by writing, or even by reading fiction, that we all see life as sleep-walkers; and fiction, like any other art, gives us momentarily to wonder whether life is not more than that which we believe it to be."

Shortly after this, Gale was involved in a political fray between the Governor of Wisconsin Phillip La Follette, whose father Robert (Fighting Bob) La Follette and the Progressive movement she had come to believe in, and the president of the University of Wisconsin, Glenn Frank, a man whom Gale had recommended to the post. The struggle consumed nearly all of her energy and time for over a year. Afterward, she spent several weeks on a tour of Japan in order to recover from the ordeal.

Zona Gale was 64 years old in the summer of 1938 and had reached a certain graceful serenity in her life. Always fragile in health, Gale fell ill in the late autumn of 1938. A few days before Christmas she went to the doctor and was hospitalized in Chicago. Pneumonia had set in and on Dec. 27 she died, moving toward that "something more" that she had always coveted.

### ZONA GALE: SELECTED READING
- *Miss Lulu Bett/Birth* by Zona Gale, Badger Books Inc./ Waubesa Press, 1994.
- *Bridal Pond,* Alfred A. Knopf, New York, 1930. 261 pp.
- *Friendship Village,* MacMillan & Company, New York, 1908. 323 pp.
- *Neighborhood Stories,* MacMillan & Company, New York, 1914. 306 pp.
- *Yellow Genitans and Blue,* D. Appleton-Century Company, New York, 1927.Z
- *Papa La Fleur,* D. Appleton-Century Company, New York, 1933.
- *Portage, Wisconsin and Other Essays,* Alfred A. Knopf, New York, 1921.
- *The Loves of Pelleas and Etarre,* The MacMillan Company, New York, 1907. 341 pp.
- *Faint Perfume,* Samuel French, New York, 1934. 126 pp.
- *Light Woman,* D. Appleton-Century Company, New York, 1937. 221 pp.
- *Still Small Voice: The Biography of Zona Gale* by August Derleth, D. Appleton & Co., 1940.

# ALDO LEOPOLD

No other Wisconsin writer has written a more important book about Wisconsin — its land and its people — than Aldo Leopold in *A Sand County Almanac.*

Aldo Leopold was not a writer by trade; he wrote essays, papers, reports and brochures having to do with his career as a teacher, scientist and official in various posts in the U.S. Department of Forestry and Game Management. But he knew how to craft his words carefully to create a tapestry of images and associations to get his points across.

His literary legacy amounted to just three books, some 500 published articles, reports, handbooks, newsletters and reviews as well as 500 unpublished pieces. Yet just one book, *A Sand County Almanac,* led to a revolution in the concept of a land ethic and cemented his reputation as a Wisconsin writer.

Aldo Leopold was born in Burlington, Iowa, in 1887 (although some sources list the year as 1886). His father, Carl, came to America in 1830 and married the daughter of a banker. Carl went on to found a furniture company that made high quality walnut desks.

Aldo turned to nature early in childhood, becoming well-versed and absorbed in woodcraft to the point where he occasionally was late to school. Carl often took young Aldo on hunting trips that evolved into life lessons on ethics and responsibility. By the time he was 15, Aldo knew what he wanted to do with his life. Yale University had just begun the nation's first forestry program, and Aldo began to prepare himself for it by leaving Burlington and attending Lawrenceville School in New Jersey, which was a training ground for future Ivy Leaguers. After 18 months, Aldo was accepted into Yale.

It was not an easy life for the young midwesterner. He suffered at times from overwork; at times from too many outside distractions. But he graduated from Yale University in 1909 with a master's degree in forestry. He joined the fledgling U.S. Forest Service. It had been organized four years earlier and the term "conservation" as we now know it was first used in 1907.

President Theodore Roosevelt had been acutely conscious of the nation's dwindling wilderness and he acted to preserve as much as possible from rapid expansion and development.

While at his first post along the Gila River in the Southwest, Leopold soon became aware that conservation not only involved trees but land as well.

In 1911, Leopold was transferred to the Carson National Forest in Albuquerque. He met beautiful 20-year-old Estelle Bergere, who lived with her family on a ranch near Santa Fe. Leopold fell in love and wooed Estelle with a determination matched only by his love for the wilderness. They were married in October 1912. On a horseback trip soon afterward, Leopold developed a case of acute nephritis and was gravely ill for several months. Aldo and Estella eventually had five children: Starker (1913), Luna (1915), Nina (1917), Carl (1919) and Estella (1927).

Leopold continued to pursue his ideas of wilderness preservation. In 1919, he was the chief of operations for the Southwestern District and responsible for over 20 million acres of national forests. In 1924, however, he accepted a transfer to Madison, Wisconsin, as associate director of the U.S. Forest Products Laboratory, the principal research unit of the Forest Service. His book, *Game Management,* written over a two-year period in the early 1930s, opened a new chapter in professional wildlife management. It still is absorbing reading today.

In 1933, Leopold became the first appointee to the newly created chair of game management at the University of Wisconsin. One of his enduring achievements was the creation in 1934 of the University of Wisconsin Arboretum, a natural woods in Madison. Today, nearly 70 years later, one can walk through the Arboretum and marvel at the legacy Aldo Leopold has left to us.

In 1935, Leopold bought an abandoned farm outside Baraboo, Wisconsin. This became the Leopold family's re-

**Aldo Leopold. Photo by Robert Grilley, courtesy of** *Wisconsin State Journal/Capital Times* **newsroom library.**

treat from the pressure and hubbub of city life. It was christened "The Shack," and the family worked together to restore the land and trees that had been destroyed by drought and neglect. Later, visitors to The Shack marveled at the acres of pines whispering in the wind, the many varieties of bushes and shrubs that harbored small wildlife. It was here at The Shack that Aldo Leopold began putting together the fragments that would become *A Sand County Almanac.*

Leopold began working on *A Sand County Almanac* in 1941. He completed a manuscript in three sections:

• The Almanac itself, which consisted of direct accounts of his observations on nature and wildlife;

• "Sketches Here and There," which chronicled some of his early adventures as well as later trips into the wilderness;

• "The Upshot," which consolidated his thoughts and offered a practical plan for wilderness preservation and conservation.

In late 1947, Leopold sent the manuscript to several publishers including Alred Knopf. Knopf rejected it, advising Leopold to rewrite it completely. Leopold's son, Luna, consulted an editor at Oxford University Press who appeared interested.

On April 14, 1948, Leopold was delighted to learn that the book had been accepted for publication.

Two days later, Leopold and his family left for The Shack, where he once again labored over his pine seedlings and tended to his morning ritual observations. He often would rise at 3:30 a.m. and sit outside, notebook and pencil ready for the first bird-song to grace the pre-dawn sky. On April 21, he saw smoke rising from the marshes to the east. Leopold, his wife and daughter Estella, hurried to the scene. He went to help fight the fire, but collapsed and died of a heart attack, then the fire passed over him.

*A Sand County Almanac* was published in 1949. Today, the Aldo Leopold Foundation continues the work of helping to preserve our natural environment. The Shack still stands amidst a mature crop of pines, and visitors from around the world are introduced to the enduring legacy of Aldo Leopold.

## ALDO LEOPOLD: SELECTED READING

- *A Sand County Almanac,* with essays on conservation from Round River, Ballantine, 1970.
- *Round River: From the journals of Aldo Leopold,* edited by Luna B. Leopold. Oxford University Press, 1953.
- *The Sand Country of Aldo Leopold,* edited by Anthony Wolff, Sierra Club, 1973.
- *Aldo Leopold's Wilderness: Selected Early Writings,* edited by David E. Brown and Neil B. Carmony, Stackpole, 1990.
- *The River of the Mother of God and Other Essays,* edited by Susan L. Flader and J. Baird Callicott, University of Wisconsin Press, 1991.
- *Aldo Leopold: A Fierce Green Fire* by Marybeth Lorbiecki, Falcon Publishing, 1996.

# ELLA WHEELER WILCOX

The poems of Ella Wheeler Wilcox are in the popular style of the 1870s and 1880s when "the Fireside Poets" — Henry Wadsworth Longfellow, John Greenleaf Whittier, William Cullen Bryant, and Oliver Wendell Holmes among others — composed rhyming quatrains that "raised hope and made the blood sing." While many of these poems today seem outdated and even juvenile, in Ella's time they would be recited wherever the public would gather for an important occasion.

As one critic noted in reviewing her book *Poems of Pleasure,* she "speaks to the rhythm of a young and growing nation."

Ella Wheeler was born on Nov. 5, 1850, in Johnstown, Rock County, Wisconsin. Before Ella was 2, the Wheeler family — her parents, Marcus and Sarah, and three older children — moved to Dane County and settled in a farmhouse in the town of Westport. Her mother always believed that Ella would be a writer, even before birth. Ella wrote a novel on scrap paper at the age of 9. Ella's reading habits were influenced by the magazines to which the family subscribed — *Peterson's, Godey's* and *Demarest's Magazine* — and the New York newspapers.

As she is quoted in *The Worlds and I*: "This emotional literature... caused me to live in a world quite apart from that of my commonplace farm environment, where the post office was five miles distant, mail came only two or three times a week."

Ella went to the University of Wisconsin in Madison already a published writer, but her distaste for schoolwork and desire to use all her time in writing grew so strong that she left after one semester. "Everything was material to me in those days — the wind, the bees, the birds, and every word dropped by my elders in conversation which had a possible romantic trend." The area around the communites of Windsor, Westport, Token Creek and Waunakee (which used to be called Leicester) was fodder for her early poems.

A bright, vivacious young woman, Ella had many suitors, including the poet James Whitcomb Riley. After the University of Wisconsin, Ella took a job as editor of a magazine in Milwaukee, but it folded after just three months. While in Milwaukee, though, Ella became part of a club called "OBJ," which meant "Oh, Be Joyful." She also became involved in the temperance movement and at the age of 22 had her first book of poems published by the National Temperance Society, *Drops of Water*. Another volume, *Shells*, with more than a hundred poems, was published the following year.

Ella's first success came about with the publication of a lengthy narrative poem called "Maurine" in 1876. It was a modest success and that inspired Ella to soon after publish another book of poems, *Poems of Passion*, all of which had appeared previously in magazines. It came as a great shock to Ella that her poems were deemed immoral and obscene. Her collection was rejected by one publisher on the basis of morality and newspapers reported that she was deemed too racy. One poem, based on a Theophile Gautier short story, was thought to have been about Ella's own experiences.

The lines from Ella's best known poem, "Solitude" came to her when Ella saw a young woman "clothed in deepest black... the bride of a year, the widow of a week, a lovely girl whom I had last seen radiant with happiness." The first four lines came immediately and when Ella recited them to some friends, one said, "Ella, if the rest of your poem measures up to the beginning, you will have a literary masterpiece!"

*Laugh and the world laughs with you,*
*Weep and you weep alone.*
*For the sad old earth must borrow its mirth,*
*It has trouble enough of its own.*

In 1883, while shopping in a Milwaukee store, Ella met

**A young Ella Wheeler Wilcox. Photo courtesy of Wisconsin Historical Society.**

Robert Wilcox, a businessman from Connecticut. After a year, they were married. To Ella's surprise, Wilcox, beneath his urbane and steadfast manner, had a great interest in matters of spirituality and reincarnation, which Ella had studied from an early age. Ella and Robert moved from Wisconsin to Meriden, Conn. Her literary output continued to grow. When *An Ambitious Man* was published in 1896, Ella had already written 13 books.

Upon learning that she was pregnant, Ella's hopes soared. Assuming that the baby would be a girl, she and Robert referred to it as "Winifred" and constantly included Winifred as a live person in their conversation and letters. The baby was a boy who lived just 12 hours and the sorrow of Ella and Robert lingered for the rest of their lives.

Ella and Robert lived in New York for about 19 years but always spent their summers at "The Bungalow" on the Connecticut seashore. There, she had many visitors, including Edwin Markham and Theodosia Garrison. Zona Gale also visited, and Ella recounts the first time she met Zona, who as a young girl appeared at the home of Judge Braley in Madison while Ella was visiting there and asked Ella if "she would look at some of her [Zona's] writings and tell her if she had talent."

In one of the most interesting chapters in her book *The Worlds and I,* Ella talks about "Lunatics I have Known." A girl from Nebraska appears one day and lives on her lawn writing letters to Ella; several men pursue her until Ella's friends begin calling her "The Lunatic's Own."

The spiritual world continued to shape Ella's life. A fortune teller once predicted that Ella would soon be surrounded by kings and queens and all manner of royalty. Ella scoffed at this, but within days she was in England to witness the funeral of Queen Victoria and her position was so close to the procession that she could have reached out and touched half the kings of the world. She was assigned to cover the funeral by an editor at Hearst Newspapers, where she wrote an advice column.

On a return voyage from the West Indies, Ella asked someone to read her tea leaves. She was told that she would stay home for a very short time and then leave again on a sea voyage that would last over a year. This came about when Ella's mother died just as Ella returned home. To recover from this loss, she and Robert took a sea voyage around the world, to Ceylon and Java, India and Japan.

Ella's views of death are some of the most striking examples of her poetry and much of it was based on her own experiences. Four times in her life up to this point she was with a person as they died.

In Jamaica, Ella met Jack London and his wife and they become good friends. Ella and Robert had become world travelers and *The Worlds and I* contains some fascinating insights into the condition of women and children in Asia,

India and Africa. Interestingly, Ella Wheeler Wilcox in 1911 seems to have been one of the first people to advocate home rule for India.

All during the winter of 1916, Robert Wilcox had been putting his affairs in order so that Ella would be able to continue after his death. He seemed to have a premonition that he was to die soon and often told Ella that if he went first, he would try to contact her from beyond and that she should look for him. His premonition came true. He caught a cold in the spring of 1917 and it developed into pneumonia. On May 21, he died in Ella's arms.

After Robert's death, Ella went to California in search of a way to contact the spirit of her husband. This was a remarkable period, Ella's own "dark night of the soul." After months of fruitless quests, Ella returned to Connecticut and there she was contacted one night by her husband via the Ouija board. In the presence of several witnesses, she brought forth information about those present that only Robert Wilcox would have known.

She often was seen as quiet and shy. When she met the California poet Joaquin Miller, he looked down at her amidst his bushy beard and six-foot four-inch frame, saying, "Why, Elly, I didn't think you were so petite and pinky; I imagined you a big-wristed girl out West milking cows."

But Ella's criticism could be biting. Once, when a critic made fun of her song/poem "Mother, Bring My Little Kitten," she replied with another verse, the title suggested by the critic, "Daddy, Do Not Drown The Puppies" but with this wicked last stanza:

*Save, oh save one puppy, daddy,*
*From a fate so dark and grim—*
*Save the very smallest puppy—*
*Make an editor of him.*

One of Ella's last books, *Sonnets of Sorrow and Triumph,* is dedicated to her late husband and reflects on Ella's own feelings.

*One of us two must sometime face existence*

*Alone with memories that but sharpen pain.*
*How pitiful, how pitiful it seems*
*To feed such hunger with but husks of dream!*

In 1919, a cancerous tumor was discovered and Ella fought it long and hard, continuing to write nearly up to the day of her death on October 30, 1919. Ella's total output included over forty books of poems, stories, and songs.

### SELECTED READING:  ELLA WHEELER WILCOX
* *Drops of Water: A Selection of Temperance Poems and Recitations,*S.T. Hammond & Co. and John Kempster & Co, London. 1872.
* *Maurine,* W.B. Conkey & Co, Chicago. 1888.
* *Poems of Passion,* Belford-Clarke Co, Chicago. 1883.
* *Perdita and Other Stories,* Ogilvie. 1886.
* *Poems of Pleasure,* Albert Whitman & Co, Chicago. 1903.
* *Three Women,* W.B. Conkey & Co, Chicago. 1897.
* *An Ambitious Man,* E. A. Weeks & Co, Chicago. 1896.
* *Sonnets of Sorrow and Triumph,* George H. Doran & Co, New York. 1918.
* *The Worlds and I,* George H. Doran & Co, New York. 1918

# STERLING NORTH

No other writer seems to have captured the essence of youthful life in Wisconsin as Sterling North did. In books such as the award-winning *Rascal, The Wolfling, So Dear To My Heart* and *Night Outlasts The Whippoorwill,* Sterling North created the image of a solitary, independent boyhood, beset with momentarily encompassing dramas filled with joys and sorrows, but yet rising above them to continue the journey towards tomorrow.

Sterling North was born in 1906 near Lake Koshkonong in southern Wisconsin, but his family soon moved to Edgerton, Wisconsin, where he spent most of his childhood years. His father, David North, was an easy-going man. He was college educated but, instead of concentrating on a single profession, he worked at various trades with occasional successes and failures. Sterling was born when his father was 42, and David North lived to be almost a centenarian, dying seven months short of his 100th birthday. But Sterling's mother died when he was 7. With his permissive father, Sterling soon became an unusually independent boy, capable of taking care of himself.

In his teens, Sterling was stricken with polio, and his recovery was given added impetus by Gladys Buchanan, whom he later married. North went to the University of Chicago where he began his writing career, sending poetry to national magazines and later won the Witter Bynner Inter-collegiate Poetry Prize. His first short story sale was to Marianne Moore for her magazine *The Dial. Poetry* magazine awarded him the Young Poet's Prize.

But college was expensive, so North began working at the *Chicago Daily News.* In the next office was Carl Sandburg, with whom North became friends. North would later work for *The New York Post* and the *New York World Telegram and Sun*. During this period in New York, North wrote *So Dear To My Heart*, the first of the books about childhood in Wisconsin. This story about a young boy who adopts and raises a black-wool lamb became a best-seller and was later filmed by Walt Disney. It is a terrific story, full of surprises that tug at the reader's emotions.

North had written and published several books before *So Dear To My Heart* and in these he introduces us to the town of "Brailsford Junction," a fictional Edgerton. In *Plowing on Sunday* and *Night Outlasts The Whippoorwill* there are recurring characters and a steady time line from the past to the present. Early Ann Sherman (later to become Early Ann Brailsford) is a memorable character in both books: She's a girl with a mysterious past who is as self-contained and independent as North was.

North also wrote a number of biographies and nature sketches, two of which are recommended reading. *Hurry, Spring!* delivers sketches of nature in an easy style. He gives us a description and history of wildlife in the early spring. *Thoreau of Walden Pond* is an interesting and nicely illustrated story/biography of Henry David Thoreau. For young readers, it gives idealized character sketches of Thoreau and other major figures living in and near Concord, Massachusetts: Emerson, Hawthorne and Bronson Alcott.

It was the publication of *Rascal* in 1963 that cemented Sterling North's name in the pantheon of Wisconsin writers. *Rascal* is the only truly autobiographical book that North wrote and its heartwarming depiction of North's boyhood and his raising of a pet raccoon almost instantly captured the hearts of young and old alike. *Rascal*, subtitled *A Memoir of a Better Era*, is filled with memorable people and places, most of which can still be seen in and around Edgerton.

To date, *Rascal* has sold over two-and-a-half million copies and has been published in more than twenty languages. It was filmed by Walt Disney in 1969 and was a huge success. *Rascal* is one of three books by Sterling North still in print, published by E.P. Dutton & Co. (the other two are

**Sterling North and friends. Photo courtesy of *Wisconsin State Journal/Capital Times* newsroom library.**

*The Wolfling* and the biography *Abe Lincoln*).

After *Rascal,* Sterling North wrote just one more book, *The Wolfling,* published in 1969 at the same time *Rascal* was in the movie theaters. *The Wolfling,* described by the author as "A Documentary Novel of the 1870's," portrays a young boy, based on North's father, who discovers and raises a young wolf pup. The book is rife with historical details, including a biographical section devoted to the great Swedish-American naturalist Thure Kumlein, who was a neighbor of the Norths on Lake Koshkonong.

North's three most popular novels all had the same theme — the interaction between a young boy and an animal he attempts to raise. In these works, North gives us a most enjoyable and honest account of man and nature at home together.

Sterling North died in 1974. He had lived in rural New Jersey for many years in a house that was as open to the foxes, deer and, of course, raccoons from a nearby national park as it was to those human visitors who came to learn all about Rascal.

Since North's death, he has been pretty much forgotten except by people in Edgerton. In 1989, The Sterling North Society was founded to preserve and promote the legacy North left to Edgerton in his books. Today, those who visit Edgerton see a large sign at the edge of town with a portrait of Rascal, and the Edgerton Public Library has a reading room with a glass display of North's books in several languages.

The Sterling North Society has published a brochure with a guide map to the sites in *Rascal* and *The Wolfling*. The society also restored North's boyhood home, where Rascal wandered in and out as a young Sterling North read detective magazines. Eventually the house will become a museum open to the public.

Before I thought of writing about Sterling North, and having never read him before, I bought a paperback copy of *The Wolfling*. Taped inside the cover of the book was this newspaper article:

RASCAL BACK? . . .

You don't believe in reincarnation? well, consider the incident that happened last week at the Stanley Pierce farm, located about 10 miles west of Fort Atkinson off of Highway 106. The family's youngest member, Chip, 4, was playing, with a kitten in the farm home kitchen, when, up through the basement door and into the room waddled a raccoon. According to the family, the furry creature looked around, walked through several rooms and finally stretched out on the davenport, very much at home. Chip and one of his older sisters, Jennifer, herded the raccoon out the kitchen door but not without a little resistance, as the animal reportedly seemed to prefer the basement to the out-of-doors. A day later the family discovered the animal curled up behind their car. Unusual? Well, you might think so when you consider that Sterling North, the author of *Rascal,* a memoir to North's pet boyhood raccoon, spent many of his young days on that same farm.

## STERLING NORTH: RECOMMENDED READING

- *The Pedro Gorino.* Houghton, 1929.
- *Plowing on Sunday.* MacMillan, 1934.
- *Night Outlasts The Whippoorwill.* MacMillan, 1936
- *Seven Against The Years.* MacMillan, 1939.
- *Speak of the Devil.* Doubleday, 1945.
- *So Dear To My Heart.* Doubleday, 1947, 1968.
- *Thoreau of Walden Pond.* Houghton, 1959.
- *Rascal: A Memoir of A Better Era.* Dutton, 1963. Avon, 1969.
- *Hurry, Spring!* Dutton, 1966.
- *The Wolfling; a Documentary Novel of the 1870's.* Dutton, 1969.

# EDNA FERBER

Edna Ferber wrote big novels. Big in character, big in scope, and big in sheer wordage. She was a product of her time, when there was so much was happening, so much to record. It was a time of rapid expansion and rapid invention, when America was pushing past England and Germany as the industrial capital of the world. Edna Ferber tried to capture all of it.

She wrote books encompassing every major region in the United States, from New England to the Mississippi River, from Oklahoma to Alaska (when Alaska was still a raw, untamed territory and not a state). She wrote about the people, the mixture of all nationalities that made up the great melting pot that was early 20th century America. She wrote about Poles, Swedes, Germans, Irish, Mexicans, and gave them each a uniquely identifiable character, yet rarely did she descend into the stereotypes prevalent in the literature that flourished then.

Edna Ferber wrote only a few books and short stories with Wisconsin themes. Chicago, for many years, was the center of her literary house, and few authors have ever written as honestly and forthrightly of Chicago and its citizens.

Edna Ferber's mother, Julia Neumann, was raised in Chicago and developed a reputation as "a high-spirited, harumscarum girl."

Julia married Jacob Ferber, a Hungarian immigrant who brought with him a small fortune to be invested in business. The Ferbers left Chicago and settled in Kalamazoo, Michigan where Jacob opened a dry goods store. There, on August 15 1887, Edna Ferber was born — the younger of two daughters.

When Edna was 3, the Ferbers left Kalamazoo and returned briefly to Chicago before moving to Ottumwa, Iowa. In the seven years Edna lived in Ottumwa, she was exposed to the harsher side of life.

She saw grim-faced Welsh miners, drab women, and bigotry in every form; she once witnessed a lynching where a man was hanged from a lamppost. Religious revivals came frequently to Ottumwa, and these spectacles began a life-long aversion in Edna to public displays of worship.

When Edna was 11, the Ferbers moved to Appleton and there Edna spent her adolescence. She was an outgoing, somewhat pudgy girl who yearned to be an actress *a la* Sarah Bernhardt.

At seventeen, Edna became the first female reporter on the *Appleton Crescent* newspaper. Her experiences at this paper would form the basis of several of her novels, most notably her first, *Dawn O'Hara: or The Girl Who Laughed.*

Her first short story sale gave evidence of Edna Ferber's very businesslike attitude and approach to writing. "The Homely Heroine" was sold to Everyman's Magazine for $50.60, but Ferber was furious at what she thought was a niggardly sum. She never sent them another story.

After eighteen months at the *Appleton Crescent*, Ferber moved on to the *Milwaukee Journal.* Here she grew to hate the sound of one person's name who was forever being held up as an example of reporter-turned-successful-writer. That name was Zona Gale. Ferber and Zona Gale met but once, which Ferber self-consciously records in her autobiography, *A Peculiar Treasure,* published in 1939.

After three years at the *Milwaukee Journal,* Edna had to quit because of ill health. Never very healthy, Ferber suffered from anemia much of her life. Oddly, she functioned much better at high altitudes, and in later years she would take yearly sojourns to Colorado, New Mexico and the Pyrenees in Spain.

Edna Ferber's first successes as a writer came about through a series of short stories featuring the first modern businesswoman, Emma McChesney. Magazines would pay up to a thousand dollars for each McChesney story, and Ferber wrote enough of them to fill three volumes.

For the next several years Edna Ferber alternated be-

tween Chicago and New York. In both cities she had a congenial circle of friends, but she never married and in later
life would write poignantly of her situation. She was very
aware of her Jewish roots and made it a point to depict the
customs and fashions of foreign immigrants in her work.

From *Dawn O'Hara,* Edna Ferber turned next to *Fanny
Herself* which was the story of a Jewish family in a small
Wisconsin town. Ferber kills off the character of Molly
Brandeis in the middle of the story because "she was tak-
ing too much attention away from the heroine." Ferber
would do the same thing twenty years later in the novel
*Come and Get It.*

All of Ferber's novels revolve around strong people and,
as Ferber herself admitted: "Plot is something that doesn't
interest me. Character I find absorbing. My novels are usually character-strong and plotweak."

World War I strengthened Edna Ferber's sense of Jewish
identity. During this period she wrote mainly short stories
about normal people doing normal things amidst an aura
of fear and uncertainty.

One of the stories, "The Farmer in the Dell," depicts the
Chicago market district, and Ferber expanded on that in
the novel *So Big* in early 1923. *So Big,* a story of an English
girl married into a Dutch farm, was Edna's first great seller
— over 323,000 copies. It also won Edna Ferber the Pulitzer
Prize for literature in 1924.

Edna Ferber said about the writing of *So Big:* "The last
page of *So Big* had been written before the first page was
started. This same thing, later, was true of *Show Boat* and
*Cimarron.* It usually is true of any first-rate piece of work I
do. If that last page writes itself before the story is well
begun then the story itself will have inevitability."

Edna settled into what seemed to be a routine: She wrote
a novel, then short stories, then a play in an almost unbro-
ken sequence. The plays were usually adaptations of the
novels or short stories and on occasion she would collabo-
rate with George Kaufman.

The genesis for Ferber's most successful book came
about during the frenzied rehearsal for one of her plays.

Winthrop Ames, who was producing Ferber's play "Old Man Minick," dourly joked that "they might as well hire on a show boat." Edna Ferber asked, "What's a show boat?"

"A floating theatre," she was told and instantly the idea for the novel *Show Boat* glimmered and took form. Few works of American literature have been adapted as well as *Show Boat.* It was made into a land-

A young Edna Ferber. Photo courtesy of Wisconsin Historical Society. (WHi-11476)

mark film with musical scores by Jerome Kern and lyrics by Oscar Hammerstein. It has played on stage and been recorded on vinyl LPs. The songs, including "Ol' Man River," are still performed today.

Like Mark Twain, Edna Ferber captured an important part of American history and made it come alive with excitement and drama. Edna Ferber's place in the history of American literature was now secure. From this point on, her novels would automatically become best-sellers and transpose into cinema classics. *So Big, Cimarron, Come and Get It, Giant,* and her best-known play, *Dinner At Eight,* were all made into films featuring such cinematic stars as Walter Brennan, Frances Farmer, James Dean, Elizabeth Taylor, and Walter Pidgeon.

Other Ferber novels are: *Great Son,* a story of Seattle and the Great Northwest; *American Beauty,* which tells of the transition of New England farms, especially tobacco farms, from English owners to Polish immigrants; and *Ice Palace,* set in Alaska.

Edna Ferber's last book was *A Kind of Magic,* a book of non-fiction published in 1963. She was then 76. Five years later, she died of cancer. Her obituary in the *New York Times* eloquently spoke of her career: "Her books were not profound, but they were vivid and had a sound sociological basis. She was among the best-read novelists in the nation, and critics of the 1920's and 1930's did not hesitate to call her the greatest American woman novelist of her day."

### SELECTED READING: EDNA FERBER

- *Dawn O'Hara or The Girl Who Laughed,* Stokes, 1911.
- *Buttered Side Down,* Stokes, 1912.
- *Fanny Herself,* Stokes, 1917.
- *So Big,* Doubleday, 1924.
- *Show Boat,* Doubleday, 1926.
- *American Beauty,* Doubleday, 1931.
- *Come and Get It,* Doubleday, Doran, 1935; Prairie Oak Press, 1992.
- *Nobody's In Town /Trees Die At The Top,* Doubleday, Doran, 1938.
- *A Peculiar Treasure,* Doubleday, Doran, 1939.
- *Great Son,* Doubleday, Doran, 1945.
- *One Basket,* Simon and Schuster, 1947.
- *Ferber: A Biography,* by Julia Goldsmith Gilbert, Doubleday & Co. New York, 1978.

# AUGUST DERLETH

No survey on Wisconsin literature can be complete without acknowledging the tremendous impact August Derleth has had on the literary landscape of his home state. The numbers are staggering. More than 150 books published during his lifetime (and at least twenty have been published since his death, many containing previously uncollected material). Over 3,000 poems. Hundreds of short stories, book reviews, nature studies, daily columns and much more. Simply stated: August Derleth did it all—and he wrote about it.

August Derleth was born on February 24, 1909, in Sauk City, Wisconsin, the only son of William and Rose Derleth. He had an older sister, Hildred. William Derleth was a blacksmith, a strong, tall, taciturn man, proud of his Germanic heritage. Young August's early years were spent roaming the fields and woods, the hills and bluffs surrounding Sauk City and the Wisconsin River. An impulsive, robust lad, he grew up with a circle of friends with whom he fished, swam on the well-known Bare Ass beach, and visited at their homes, most of which were near the *Freie Gemiende* (or FreeThinker's) Park. Derleth had little interest in hunting or sports like baseball and football. His idea of exercise was to take long hikes. Though he occasionally rode a bicycle, Derleth preferred to walk where he could stop and observe whatever caught his interest. He developed a critical eye for noting fine details that crop up time and again in his writings.

Derleth came to reading at an early age, influenced by his mother. He read voraciously and continued to do so all his life, despite his demanding schedule as a writer, editor, publisher and teacher. He also indulged in other activities, including taking the month of May off for a favorite pastime — hunting morel mushrooms.

By the time he had graduated from St. Aloysius Parochial School, Derleth knew that he wanted to become a writer. In high school he teamed up with his friend Mark Schorer, who also wanted to be a writer, and they rented a cabin for a summer. Every day Derleth and Schorer would sit in the cabin pounding away on a battered typewriter to produce mostly horror stories. By this time, Derleth had been reading a pulp magazine called *Weird Tales* that featured stories by H.P. Lovecraft, a reclusive writer living in Providence, Rhode Island. Derleth began corresponding with Lovecraft in early 1926, and their voluminous exchanges lasted until Lovecraft's death in 1937. Spurred by Lovecraft's interest in his stories, Derleth began submitting tales that he and Schorer had written to *Weird Tales*, which accepted several and paid Derleth between $8 and $12 per story.

Derleth attended the University of Wisconsin and graduated from there in 1930 with a bachelor's degree in English. While in Madison, Derleth lived in an apartment (since torn down) on West Johnson Street and came under the guidance of novelist and well-known professor Helen Constance White. He also at this time began writing the autobiographical novel that would become *Evening In Spring*. Another pastime was the writing of mysteries. Derleth had learned that Sir Arthur Conan Doyle planned not to write any more Sherlock Holmes detective mysteries. Derleth then wrote to Doyle asking if this was true. When Doyle answered yes, young Derleth created his own character based on Sherlock Holmes and called him Solar Pons. The stories were also set in London, England, but Pons didn't live on Baker Street. His residence was located at 7B Praed Street.

After graduation, Derleth took a job as the editor of *Mystic Magazine*, which specialized in "true tales of the paranormal." He moved to Minneapolis but, as he wrote later in the prologue to *Walden West,* he missed his hometown of Sac Prairie.

And thus, in 1931, after four months in Minneapolis, Derleth returned to Sac Prairie and, except for brief excursions, stayed there the rest of his life.

In the early 1930s, Derleth began to write what he described as a series of 50 books of both prose and poetry to chronicle the life and history of Sauk City and Prairie du Sac. This became *Sac Prairie Saga*, which totaled 20 books at the time of his death. Included in the *Sac Prairie Saga* are *Walden West, Evening In Spring, Village Year, Sac Prairie People* and several volumes of poetry. These are among Derleth's best known works.

Having already written several Solar Pons mysteries, Derleth learned in 1933 of a new publisher, Loring & Mussey, that was seeking manuscripts. Derleth wrote *Murder Stalks The Wakely Family*, set in Sac Prairie and featuring Judge Ephraim Peck. The book was published in 1934, his first book. The next year, Derleth followed with two more Judge Peck mysteries, *Sign of Fear* and *Three Who Died*. Also in 1935, Loring & Mussey published the first book in *Sac Prairie Saga, Place of Hawks*, containing three novellas written around the madness and decay of three generations of a Sac Prairie family.

H.P. Lovecraft's death in 1937 hit Derleth hard. In many ways Lovecraft had been Derleth's mentor, often sending the 28-year-old writer his own handwritten manuscripts for Derleth to type up prior to submitting them. At the time of Lovecraft's death, Derleth had signed with Charles Scribner's Sons. His editor was the famed Maxwell Perkins (who had guided F. Scott Fitzgerald, Ernest Hemingway and Thomas Wolfe) and it was a stormy business relationship. Derleth hated revising, but Perkins was a staunch adherent of the blue pencil. But Perkins knew how to bring out the best in Derleth. All during 1936 Derleth had worked on his first serious novel, *Still is the Summer Night*, and it was published just before Lovecraft died. One of Lovecraft's final letters praises the authenticity of the setting and the characters. *Still is the Summer Night* tells the story of the tragic love triangle between Alton Halder, his wife Julie, and his brother Ratio. Derleth first displays here the timeless charm and sense of a recaptured past that would become the primary theme of much of *Sac Prairie Saga*.

Derleth's first poetry collection *Hawk on the Wind* was published in 1938, as was the second book in *Sac Prairie*

*Saga, Wind Over Wisconsin.* This was also the novel that
acquainted me with August Derleth's non-supernatural fiction writing — and later was a primary consideration in
my moving to Wisconsin after graduating from college in
1988: I wanted to see "Derleth country." And *Wind Over
Wisconsin* remains one of my favorite August Derleth books.
Set in the Sac Prairie area in the 1830s, the story finds Baron
Chalfonte Pierneau living with his wife Adrienne and two
children in a splendid limestone house on top of a hill above
the Wisconsin River. Pierneau is a fur trapper and trader
who is concerned about the trade dying out. He has two
other men to help him operate his land and business,
Aristide Clement and Dave Kerry. A visit by two trappers,
LaPiage and Souligne, concerns Chalfonte enough to visit
the new settlement of Prairie du Chien and see Hercules
Dousman, then a rising young clerk in the employ of John
Jacob Astor. Chalfonte's idealism is harshly balanced
against Dousman's stolid pragmatism, yet the two become
friends.

Indian trouble breaks out as a result of what would later
be called the Black Hawk War. Pierneau has been friends
with the Sac chief Black Hawk, and his farm is close to the
scene of the Battle of Wisconsin Heights. When renegade
Indians attack his house, Adrienne is shot in the leg by a
poisoned arrow. What follows is a heart-wrenching account
of Pierneau comforting his dying wife in her final moments
of life.

The year 1939 proved to be pivotal for Derleth. As the
books and stories and poetry continued to flow from his
typewriter, he began looking around for a place to build his
own home. On the west edge of Sauk City, he bought from
the Lueders sisters, Augusta and Carlotta, ten acres and
the house in which they had lived for over seventy years.
Franz Lueders had been a naturalist and scientist in Germany, and he had brought over many plants and young
trees so that the Lueders land featured an astonishing va-
riety of tree and plant life, especially suited to Derleth's
own love of nature. Tearing down the old house, Derleth
hired Chicago architect Leo Weissenborn who, along with

William Derleth, built the house known today as "Place of Hawks." Frank Lloyd Wright, with whom Derleth had struck up a friendship, came to see the house and remarked, "August, you've built a barn!" to which Derleth replied, "That's only proper — a bull will be living in it."

The other significant event of that year was the founding of Arkham House. Upon hearing of H.P. Lovecraft's death in March of 1937, Derleth vowed to see his late friend's writings preserved in book form. Along with fellow writer Donald Wandrei, Derleth created Arkham House (the name is taken from the fictional Arkham, Massachusetts, a village featured in several of Lovecraft's macabre tales). In 1939, *The Outsider and Others* was published and sold for $3.50. Sales were slow, but Derleth was unperturbed. He contacted several other of what had become known as "the Weird Tales circle" of writers: Frank Belknap Long, Henry Kuttner, Clark Ashton Smith, Robert E. Howard (who had committed suicide in 1930 but whose father was still alive) and others and gradually he published their works in book form as well. Arkham House became the first specialty publishing house devoted to science fiction, fantasy and the macabre. Arkham House still operates today out of the same warehouse next to Derleth's home. Though recent competitors have sliced into the market, Arkham retains a healthy reputation among collectors.

*Bright Journey* was August Derleth's first novel in what was to become the "Wisconsin Saga." These are historical novels about authentic personages, what Derleth would call "fictional biographies." Hercules Dousman, whom we first met in *Wind Over Wisconsin*, was Wisconsin's first millionaire. After getting his start as a clerk, Dousman would eventually take over the declining fur business but would also be instrumental in promoting agricultural practices and the railroad. Dousman fell in love with his business partner Joe Rolette's wife, Jane. After several years, Rolette dies and Dousman marries Jane and he builds for her the famous house in Prairie du Chien known as Villa Louis.

In 1940, Derleth branched out into writing a non-fictional biography about a fellow Wisconsin writer he had grown

**August Derleth. Photo courtesy of *Wisconsin State Journal/Capital Times* newsroom library.**

to like and respect. She was Zona Gale, from Portage, some thirty miles northeast of Sauk City. Zona Gale had died in 1938 and Derleth had written a long poem called "Elegy: On A Flake Of Snow" in remembrance. Now came *Still, Small Voice: The Biography of Zona Gale*. In their writings both Derleth and Gale eloquently captured the appeal of small-town life, and these elements contributed to their mutual friendship and respect.

In 1941 came the publication of *Evening In Spring,*

Derleth's autobiographical novel of his first teenage love. The opening chapters are mixed with Derleth's nostalgic look at the Sac Prairie of the 1920s and the humorous character of Grandfather Adams, who sparkles with learned wisdom that he tries to impart to the impulsive Steven Grendon, Derleth's youthful alter-ego. Steve has fallen in love with Margery Estabrook, yet Steve is from a Catholic family while Margery's parents are staunchly Lutheran. The town itself becomes an adversary in Steve's quest to win Margery's love, but early in the book it didn't seem to matter.

In 1941, Derleth published *Village Year,* the first of his Sac Prairie Journals. These contain short nostalgic, witty, true-to-life observations of the people and environs of Sac Prairie. Here we meet several characters who make Sac Prairie the microcosm and melting pot that it was in Derleth's youth. People like Barney Merkel, who at age 97 walked out into a blizzard one day and, after a frenzied search by the townsfolk and police, returned home saying that he had "seen a bit of the country." People like Andy Weber, whose colorful sayings pepper his speech— "By gosh all fish hooks!" And Derleth's two lifelong companions, Karl Ganzlin and Hugo Schwenker, who accompany Derleth on his excursions around Sac Prairie and into the country to admire the fall colors of the Baraboo bluffs.

But Derleth didn't have much time left to observe such things. On December 7, 1941, the Japanese bombed Pearl Harbor and America entered World War II. The war produced a profound change in Derleth's native Sac Prairie.

Anyone who travels along Highway 12 north of Sauk City, heading toward the rising Baraboo Hills in the distance will notice a large, sprawling complex off to the right, looking like some small industrial village surrounded by a barbed-wire fence. This is what remains of the Badger Ordnance and Ammunition Plant that was built during the 1930s to support the war effort. In order to build the plant, dozens of area farmers were moved off their land. In some cases, land had been in the family for three generations.

This was anathema to Derleth's pacifistic nature. Derleth

was in favor of capital punishment, and he was first and foremost tied to the land. Derleth vigorously railed against the displacement of the farmers, and to him the ammunition plant was an eyesore. Always keenly interested in politics, Derleth was one of the first to see the dangers inherent in the rise of Wisconsin Senator Joe McCarthy. He initiated a "Joe Must Go" campaign and helped Leroy Gore fight the rising tide of McCarthyism in the early 1950s.

During the war years, Derleth continued to produce books, including three Judge Peck novels, four books of poetry, a couple of illustrated children's books and three novels in *Sac Prairie Saga* — *Sweet Genevieve, Shadow of Night* and *The Shield of the Valiant*, his last novel for Scribner's. His relations with Maxwell Perkins had cooled to the point that Derleth no longer had a ready ear with the New York publisher. He had by then found another publisher, Stanton & Lee, in part to take the place of Scribner's as an outlet for his serious work.

By the late 1940s, Arkham House had taken over much of Derleth's time. He had been running the business by himself; Donald Wandrei had moved to Minneapolis. Arkham's books ensured a steady source of income, yet Derleth remained heavily in debt for much of his life. He often said that he was obligated to write what he called his "entertainments" so as to keep his other activities afloat.

This had been one of the reasons for the split with Perkins, who wanted Derleth to concentrate strictly on *Sac Prairie Saga* books.

In 1951 August Derleth had another interest in his life: romance. Always popular with the young women of Sauk City and Prairie du Sac, Derleth casually flirted with several women and some were the subjects of poetry. Derleth had earlier been engaged a short time to Marcia Lee Masters, daughter of the noted poet Edgar Lee Masters, but the engagement was broken off after a few months. His writing schedule did not allow time for a serious relationship. That is, until the 42-year old Derleth met and was smitten by a sixteen-year-old high school girl named Sandra Winters. Because Sandra was under the legal age for marriage, Derleth had to wait two years to get married. But the knot was tied in 1953 and in due course the Derleths had two children, April Rose and Walden William. The marriage was short-lived, ending in divorce in 1959 with August Derleth gaining custody of the children.

None of this diminished Derleth's output. Between 1951 and 1958 he published 27 books ranging from history, Solar Pons mysteries and supernatural stories to poetry and one *Sac Prairie Saga* novella *(The House of Moonlight)*. Then, in 1958, Derleth began a fruitful relationship with the New York publishing firm of Duell, Sloan and Pearce, which produced fifteen books through 1966. The first of these introduced a pair of boys, Stephen Grendon and Simoleon Jones, who roamed through the streets of Sac Prairie and the hills along the Wisconsin River participating in all sorts of adventures and usually getting into trouble. The first book was *The Moon Tenders* and it remains a favorite among young readers today. Steve Grendon is August Derleth's youthful alter-ego. "Sim" Jones is Derleth's childhood friend Hugo Schwenker. Like Tom Sawyer and Huckleberry Finn, the two teenage boys build a raft and go sailing down the Wisconsin River to explore a cave near Bogus Bluff. There, they find the hidden workshop and cache of a pair of Chicago counterfeiters — and the trouble and fun ensues. Derleth would continue this formula through nine more books in what came to be called The Mill Creek Irregulars series of juvenile mysteries.

The work that is Derleth's masterpiece, *Walden West,* was published in 1961. Throughout his life, Derleth was a great admirer of Henry David Thoreau and had in 1944 published a poetry collection titled *And You, Thoreau!* He would also write a leisurely biography of Thoreau called *Concord Rebel,* and he made three trips to visit Thoreau's Walden Pond, the first in 1938.

*Walden West* presents to the reader "An Exposition on Three Related Themes: On the Persistence of Memory, On the Sounds and Odors of the Country, and Of Thoreau: the Mass of Men Lead Lives of Quiet Desperation." Derleth weaves these themes, depicting as few writers ever have just what it is that makes up the fabric of a small town and the countryside that surrounds it.

It was while hiking that Derleth learned to sharpen his powers of observation. He habitually carried a small notebook with him to jot down his observations, ideas and the frequent poem. He followed an almost unvarying route.

*Walden West* is a book to be picked up at leisure and read a few pages at a time. It is redolent of an era where time moved much more slowly and life was there to be savored.

In the 1950s and 1960s, Derleth taught courses and seminars through the University of Wisconsin Extension Program and also at the Rhinelander School for the Arts in northern Wisconsin. These courses were usually on American or Midwestern literature. A course syllabus survives listing 34 pages of books that Derleth recommended his students to read...every one of them! This often had the effect of reducing his class size dramatically.

And still the book machine continued — ten Derleth books were published in 1963 alone! Of these, two collections of his macabre short fiction stand out, *Lonesome Places* and *Mr. George and Other Odd Persons*. Derleth also brought out several little collections of poetry through Carroll Coleman's Prairie Press, based in Iowa City, Iowa. His relationship with Duell, Sloan and Pearce ended with the death of "Cap" Pearce in 1966: Derleth found another publisher in a young man from New York City, Peter Ruber. Under the Candlelight Press imprint, Derleth established an outlet for his serious writings, including *Sac Prairie Saga.*

Derleth's health took a turn for the worse in the 1960s. He was a large man, usually weighing more than 250 pounds, and the long hours of sitting at his desk pounding on the typewriter were only slightly mitigated by the walks in the marshes. Derleth was an avid eater, a gourmand rather than a gourmet, although he loved fine food and wine. A mild coronary in 1966 set him back for awhile and he actually lost 40 pounds, but he had regained it by the time the second serious illness felled him in 1968. A simple gall bladder operation led to complications, including pneumonia and peritonitis and resulted in a hospital stay of nearly two months during which Derleth lost 53 pounds. Arkham House had grown into a three-person operation, with the Derleth children, April and Walden, helping out in their spare time.

Almost as a result of these brushes with death, Derleth's writing style changed in the late 1960s. Both his fiction and poetry became more erotic and sexual in tone. *Caitlin* (poetry) and a 1970 novella, *A House Above Cuzco,* saw Derleth rhapsodizing the ideal of the eternal female in sexually frank language.

Also in 1970, *Return To Walden West* was published. The near decade that intervened between *Walden West* and its successor also saw a change in August Derleth's writing style. With an almost premonitory awareness that his time was growing short, Derleth invested the pages of *Return to Walden West* with a darker vision and an often impassioned plea toward the conservation of his native environs. Whether he's talking about the secondary homes of his childhood — the Schorers', the Ganzlins', the Schwenkers' — or describing again the observations made on his walks through the marshes and hills, Derleth's growing impatience with the foibles of his fellow humans is evident.

On the morning of July 4, 1971, August Derleth awoke feeling so ill that he spoke of it to his mother. He went down to the post office to get the morning mail and upon returning was so weary he lay down to rest. He suffered a heart attack and was taken to the hospital, where he died at 9:55 a.m. He was 62 years old.

Derleth left much work unfinished. After his death, Arkham House continued under the editorship of James Turner, still operating out of the warehouse behind Place of Hawks. A few more Derleth titles appeared posthumously, including *Dwellers in Darkness,* another excellent collection of supernatural tales. But Derleth's standing as a major regional literary figure of the twentieth century began a steady decline.

Seven years after August Derleth's death, a man in Connecticut wandered into a used bookstore and saw *Walden*

*West.* This man, Richard Fawcett, knew Derleth solely because of Derleth's macabre writings so he was intrigued to discover that Derleth wrote other kinds of books.

After reading *Walden West,* Fawcett made a telephone call to the Sauk City Chamber of Commerce and asked if there was an August Derleth Fan Club. He was shocked to discover that none existed. So he decided to form one. He placed an advertisement in the Sauk City newspaper announcing the first meeting of the August Derleth Society would be held on July 16, 1978, at The Firehouse Restaurant in Prairie du Sac. Fawcett started up an August Derleth Society Newsletter and solicited contributions from people who knew Derleth. The society began with 248 charter members and the membership fee was $1.

Over the years the August Derleth Society continued to grow, albeit sporadically at times. A slate of officers was elected with each president serving a two-year term. The society became involved in many activities designed to perpetuate August Derleth's memory, the first being the creation of August Derleth Park along the bank of the Wisconsin River in Sauk City. Later achievements included the opening of the August Derleth Room in the Sauk City Public Library; the publication of *Remembering Derleth,* a compendium of articles and reminiscences; the designation of the Highway 12 bridge entering Sauk City as the August Derleth Bridge; the opening of "Augie's Room," a private dining area in Leystra's Restaurant in Sauk City; the sponsorship of an August Derleth Creative Writing Award presented by the University of Wisconsin English department; and many other noteworthy achievements.

The goal that eluded the August Derleth Society was to see Derleth's best works come back into print. While there were occasional Derleth books published between 1978 and 1994, it seemed inevitable that, despite his prodigious output, Derleth would become a mere footnote in twentieth-century literature.

That changed one night in 1994 when Kay Price, the executive secretary of the August Derleth Society (who was Derleth's personal secretary the final three years of his life and was with him the day before his death), received a telephone call from Dr. George Vanderburgh from Canada. Vanderburgh asked if there were any plans to reprint Derleth books. Price told him the society didn't have the money to finance such a project. Vanderburgh replied that he wanted to republish Derleth's works.

During 1995, Vanderburgh, who had earlier in the decade formed his own publishing firm specializing in books by or about Sherlock Holmes and Vincent Starrett under the Battered Silicon Dispatch Box imprint, contacted Derleth's daughter, April, and was given permission to reprint Derleth's *Collected Poems, 1937-1967.*

Vanderburgh had already been working with Peter Ruber on the Vincent Starrett books; now he discovered that Ruber had been Derleth's publisher.

Vanderburgh and Ruber formed a partnership with the goal of reprinting as many Derleth books as possible. In March 1996, *The House on the Mound* was published, and there was an immediate demand for the book, especially at Villa Louis in Prairie du Chien.

Two months later, their plans changed with the discovery of a cabinet full of Derleth material, most of it unpublished. So along with the reprinting of selected Derleth titles, Ruber and Vanderburgh had new material to consider, possibly enough for thirty more books. Since then, nineteen Derleth books have been reprinted, including *Evening In Spring* and all ten books in the Steve/Sim juvenile mystery series. New Derleth work is included in the poetry collection *In A Quiet Graveyard,* a non- fiction book *Wisconsin Writers and Writing,* a collection of short stories *Return to Sac Prairie,* and *The Lost Sac Prairie Novels.* A biography has been published and another Derleth biography is being written by University of Wisconsin — Baraboo English Professor Kenneth Grant.

On August 18, 2001, August Derleth's childhood friend Hugo Schwenker died at 92. In his will, Schwenker left the harness shop to the August Derleth Society to use as a memorial to Derleth and as a base of operations for the society to pursue its goal of keeping Derleth's memory alive.

Several decades after his death, August Derleth still holds a powerful sway over the Wisconsin literary landscape; hovering and circling above it like the totemic hawks that soar along the Wisconsin River in Sauk City— his beloved Sac Prairie.

In early 2002, April Derleth became embroiled in a dispute with local authorities over a proposed development near the Place of Hawks home.

### AUGUST DERLETH: SELECTED READING

- *Wind Over Wisconsin.* 1938, Charles Scribner's Sons, New York. 391 pp.
- *Restless is the River.* 1939, Charles Scribner's Sons, New York. 514 pp.
- *Evening in Spring.* 1941, Charles Scribner's Sons, New York. 308 pp.
- *Village year: A Sac Prairie Journal.* 1941, Coward-McCann, New York. 314 pp.
- *The Wisconsin: River of a Thousand Isles.* 1942, Farrar & Rinehart, New York. (reprinted, 1985, University of Wisconsin Press, Madison, Wisconsin. 366 pp.)
- *Shadow of Night.* 1943, Charles Scribner's Sons, New York. 354 pp.
- *Village Daybook: A Sac Prairie Journal.* 1947, Pellegrini and Cudahy, Chicago. 306 pp.
- *The Moon Tenders.* 1958, Duell, Sloan & Pearce, New York. 181 pp.
- *Walden West.* 1961, Duell, Sloan & Pearce, New York. 262 pp.
- *Lonesome Places*, 1962, Arkham House, Sauk City, Wisconsin. 198 pp.
- *Countryman's Journal.* 1963, Duell, Sloan & Pearce, New York. 215 pp.
- *Collected Poems, 1937-1967.* 1967, Candlelight Press, New York. 302 pp.
- *Return to Walden West.* 1970, Candlelight Press, New York. 233 pp.
- *Dwellers in Darkness.* 1976, Arkham House, Sauk City,

Wisconsin. 203 pp.
- *Country Matters*. 1996, Hawk & Whippoorwill Press, Sauk City, Wisconsin. 304 pp.
- *In Lovecraft's Shadow*, 1996, Mycroft & Moran, Sauk City, Wisconsin. 336 pp.
- *In a Quiet Graveyard*. 1997, Hawk & Whippoorwill Press, Sauk City, Wisconsin. 132 pp.
- *Wisconsin Writers and Writing*. 1998, Hawk & Whippoorwill Press, Sauk City, Wisconsin. 180 pp.
- *The Lost Sac Prairie Novels*, 2000, Hawk & Whippoorwill Press, Sauk City, Wisconsin. 412 pp.

# BLACK HAWK

When *The Life of Black Hawk* was published in 1834, Black Hawk himself was still alive. It was only two years after the famous so-called Black Hawk War and the old Sac chief now lived in quiet contentment in a log cabin along the Des Moines River. One of the writers of the original autobiography was a half-breed French-Canadian named Antoine LeClaire, who was given land in exchange for his services as interpreter. LeClaire later became one of the founders of the city of Davenport, Iowa.

Black Hawk was born in 1767 in a Sac village on the Rock River in what would later become the state of Illinois. He joined his first battle at the age of 15, and progressed from being considered a child to becoming a brave. Because he disobeyed an order to retreat in his next battle, Black Hawk was not allowed to lead a group of braves again until he was 19. Later that year, Black Hawk's father Pyesa was killed in a battle. Vowing revenge, on the Cherokee and Osage in particular, Black Hawk spent the next sixteen years fighting other Indian bands. He was on hand when the English took over the town of St. Louis from the Spanish. By 1811, Black Hawk had decided that there was a major difference between the Americans and the British:

"I had not made up my mind whether to join the British, or remain neutral. I had not discovered one good trait in the character of the Americans that had come to the country! They made fair promises but never fulfilled them! Whilst the British made but few—but we could always rely upon their word!" (p. 68)

Black Hawk joined the British during the War of 1812 and participated in several battles. Among them: Fort Dearborn (August 15, 1812), Frenchtown; near Lake Erie (January 22, 1813); Fort Meigs (May 1, 1813); and Fort Stephenson in Ohio (August 2, 1813). After nearly a year of fighting, Black Hawk left the British, returning to Illinois.

In 1814 Black Hawk was camping along the Mississippi

and Rock Rivers when American soldiers passed through on their way to build a fort at Prairie du Chien. Sac braves lured the boats to shore and did considerable mischief, capturing several of the soldiers. One of the soldiers in this troop was future U.S. President Zachary Taylor.

After making the mistake of signing a treaty at St. Louis in 1815, which confirmed a previous treaty of 1804 that ceded all the Sac lands, Black Hawk notes:

"We can only judge of what is proper and right by our standard of right and wrong, which differs widely from the whites, if I have been correctly informed. The whites may do bad all their lives, and then, if they are sorry for it when about to die, all is well! But with us it is different: we must continue throughout our lives to do what we conceive to be good. If we have corn and meat, and know of a family that have none, we divide with them. If we have more blankets than sufficient and others have not enough, we must give to them that want." (p. 99)

In his book, Black Hawk describes village life, especially in the late fall at harvest time and during the winter. Black Hawk describes the custom of a brave entering his intended bride's wigwam and placing a candle next to her; if she blows it out, he becomes a member of her family. William Steuber also makes note of this custom in his novel *Go Away, Thunder!*

Around 1816, Black Hawk saw his oldest son and youngest daughter die. He went into mourning but continued to lead his people. Their lands now encroached on those of the Ioway, but a peace was made between the two tribes. Not long after, Black Hawk heard talk that the Sac were to be moved west of the Mississippi River: They would have to leave their traditional land on the Rock River in Illinois.

By 1830, Black Hawk was dissatisfied with the new lands given his people. On April 5, 1832, Black Hawk began his march back to his native grounds, crossing the Mississippi River near the mouth of the lower Iowa River. What happened after this has been chronicled in many places as the Black Hawk War. Black Hawk undertook a holding action at Wisconsin Heights near Sauk City, which allowed his people

to cross the Wisconsin River on their way to the fatal climax on Aug. 2 at Bad Axe on the Mississippi River, where the Indians were defeated and Black Hawk was taken prisoner.

After his capture, Black Hawk was sent to Washington to meet with President Andrew Jackson. He was then sent on a tour of the United States and, lastly, settled down to live out his remaining years at homes along the Iowa and Des Moines rivers.

**Portrait of Chief Black Hawk. Photo courtesy of *Wisconsin State Journal/Capital Times* newsroom library.**

Black Hawk died on October 3, 1838. He was one of the first Native Americans to have his story published in a historically authenticated version.

A book that deals with the life of Black Hawk is *I Am A Man: The Indian Black Hawk* by Cyrenus Cole and published in 1938 by the State Historical Society of Iowa on the centenary of Black Hawk's death as well as the centenary of the founding of the Iowa Territory, which became a state in 1848.

### BLACK HAWK: SELECTED READING
• *Black Hawk: An Autobiography*, edited by Donald Jackson. 1955, University of Illinois Press, Urbana. 190 pp.

# CRASHING THUNDER

A photograph of Sam Blowsnake (a.k.a. Crashing Thunder) shows a vibrantly handsome young man with long flowing black hair and piercing eyes. There is a resemblance to the Sioux chief Crazy Horse, and the fine clothes he wears in the picture do not at all dispel the thought that at a moment's notice he would vault on to the back of a horse and gallop off on the warpath. While Black Hawk's autobiography was in the form of a more traditional narrative, Crashing Thunder often weaves stories and legends from Winnebago history into his own personal account.

Crashing Thunder was born around 1870 and spent his early years near Black River Falls, Wisconsin. It was still six years to the Battle of Little Big Horn a few hundred miles to the west and more than twenty before the massacre at Wounded Knee.

Fasting is an important phase in Native American life. In Crashing Thunder's account, he tells not only of his own fast but also those of his brother-in-law Thunder Cloud, his ancestor Weshigishega, and another ancestor Jobenangiwinxga, thus preserving the continuity of the narrative.

After recounting some of his devious ways as a young child — chasing after girls and eating fast so as to get more of a share — Crashing Thunder tells of the origin of the Winnebago (now called Ho-Chunk). He tells of the Earthmaker who made everything and the Four Thunderbirds who came down out of the sky.

Stories are a big part of Crashing Thunder's life. He includes several of these, most of which have a moral or an explanation at the end, such as "The Coyote and the Ghost." Ghosts play an important part as interpreters in most of these stories. They hang around both in real life and in the dream world.

Two stories reflect the role of women in Winnebago life.

A man avenges the death of his wife in the first story and in the second a man rescues his wife from the spirit world.

Crashing Thunder also relates some of his father's teachings:

"My son, it is good to die on the warpath. If you die on the warpath, you will not lose consciousness at death. You will be able to do what you please with your soul and it will always remain in a happy condition. If afterwards you wish to become reincarnated as a human being, you may do so, or you may take the form of those-who-walk-upon-the-light, the birds, or the form of any animal you please, in short." (p. 59)

Crashing Thunder's father also gave this ironic advice:

"It is not good to win at gambling. You may possibly become rich thereby but that is no life to lead. If you are blessed with luck in cards, if you are blessed with luck at gambling, you will perhaps win things and have plenty of wealth, but none of your children will live." (p. 66)

Today's Winnebago (Ho-Chunk) are heavily involved in the casino business.

There is also advice from a mother to her daughter, and Crashing Thunder tells some stories about his courting days.

When he was in his teens, Crashing Thunder went to live with his grandfather and attended school in Tomah, Wisconsin. His grandfather soon died, and Winnebago funeral customs are described. Crashing Thunder participates in a Medicine Dance and inherits the title of medicine man, but he knows he has not the heart for such a position. He travels a good deal in his early twenties, going around as part of a circus, dancing and performing for crowds. He starts drinking heavily. After hearing of his brother's murder, Crashing Thunder goes all out in debauchery. He describes himself as a large man, "six feet and two inches and about two hundred and fifty pounds." (p. 134)

He lived on a rotating basis between Black River Falls, Wittenburg and Tomah. One day, Crashing Thunder decided he had to kill a man, a Menominee, someone not of his tribe, so that he could take "war-honors." Soon after the murder, he leaves Wisconsin for Nebraska. Spending most of the summer in Nebraska, he returns later that year to help harvest the cranberries. He is arrested and spends nearly two years in jail awaiting trial for the murder. At the trial, Crashing Thunder is released and he returns to Nebraska where he falls in with some peyote-eaters. He embraces the peyote religion and the book ends there. At the time the book was written, Crashing Thunder was 45. He died in 1960.

### CRASHING THUNDER: SELECTED READING

• *Crashing Thunder: The Autobiography of an American Indian,* edited by Paul Radin. 1926, D. Appleton & Company, New York and London. 202 pp.

# MOUNTAIN WOLF
# WOMAN

Mountain Wolf Woman was born in April 1884. Her family had taken up land near Black River Falls after the U.S. government gave up trying to remove the Winnebago from Wisconsin in 1874. As a child, Mountain Wolf Woman was given her name by another woman to whom she had been given in payment after the other woman cured Mountain Wolf Woman of a dire sickness.

Often Mountain Wolf Woman's stories contain amusing parables, such as this:

"Stealing from mice is something I never did but aunt and grandmother told me about it. They would go off in the brush, in the woods, and steal wild beans from the mice. These mice know how to store things. Running back and forth, the mice carried things to a particular place. Their little trails showed the way they went into their little holes in the ground. There they gathered very many of these wild beans. Grandmother said that when a family had a lot of little boys it used to be said of the last born, the youngest one, that he is married to one of these mice. It was that boy who used to find the storehouses. That is why they used to say the little boys married little mice." (*Mountain Wolf Woman,* p. 13)

When she was 9 years old, Mountain Wolf Woman attended a school in Tomah and stayed there for two years. Later, her family moved across the state to Wittenberg where she also attended school for several more years. While still a teenager, Mountain Wolf Woman was married off to a man who soon proved to be a jealous husband. She had two children by him before she left him. Her brother, Crashing Thunder, arranged a second marriage to a Winnebago named Bad Soldier. Afterward, Mountain Wolf Woman travelled to Nebraska where she also falls into eating peyote. Her third child, a boy, was born about this time and, during one peyote session, she had visions of people fleeing before a black wind, then the figure of Jesus appears. A few years later, Mountain Wolf Woman returned to Black River Falls, having also lived among the Sioux in South Dakota.

In 1936, Bad Soldier died. Mountain Wolf Woman's account is particularly moving:

"In the evenings I used to think as I sat there, "Maybe this is not happening to me. Maybe this is not happening to me. Maybe he did not die." Children of mine died. My relatives died, father and mother. My older sister died. But it was never as bad as when my man died. "Maybe I am having a bad dream," I thought. I would pinch my arms to see if I was awake." (p. 59)

Mountain Wolf Woman had eleven children. One daughter was named White Hawk, who later moved to Waterloo, Iowa. One of her sons fought in World War II and was badly wounded in combat.

Later, Mountain Wolf Woman crossed the country from Wisconsin to Yakima, Washington on a train. In her later years, she traveled about between Nebraska and Wisconsin, visiting friends. For the interviews that resulted in her autobiography, Mountain Wolf Woman took a plane to Ann Arbor, Michigan. She died in 1960, the same year as her brother, Crashing Thunder.

**MOUNTAIN WOLF WOMAN: SELECTED READING**

• *Mountain Wolf Woman: Sister of Crashing Thunrder. The Autobiography of a Winnebago Indian.* 1961, University of Michigan Press. 142 pp.

# ROBERT BLOCH

Since 1939, Wisconsin has held a special place in the hearts of readers of science fiction, fantasy and other types of imaginative literature. It was in 1939 that Wisconsin writer August Derleth founded the publishing firm of Arkham House, at first to publish in hardcover books the stories of Howard Phillips Lovecraft (1890-1937), with whom Derleth shared a friendship via correspondence for over ten years until Lovecraft's death. Later, Derleth would expand Arkham House to include books by other writers mostly of macabre and fantasy fiction.

Among those in the state who were also writing and publishing in these various genres was Derleth's partner in Arkham House, Donald Wandrei and Donald's brother, Howard. Another was a young teenager who had just moved to Milwaukee from the Chicago area and was already corresponding with Derleth and Lovecraft. His name was Robert Bloch.

Robert Bloch was born in Chicago on April 5, 1917, the son of Stella Loeb and Raphael (Ray) Bloch. He had a younger sister named Genevieve. Bloch spent a rather idyllic childhood in the Chicago suburb of Maywood. One early childhood memory involved the death of a chicken — to which Bloch later wryly observed, "I wonder why so many of my stories involve decapitation..."

By the time he was 8, Bloch was reading Twain, Poe, Hawthorne, O. Henry, Sir Walter Scott, Washington Irving and others. Life was good in those days and involved trips to the Chicago zoo, the theater and, naturally, the movies. "The Phantom of the Opera" (1925) inspired a lifelong love for Lon Chaney's great films.

In 1927, Bloch was introduced to the magazine that would help shape his writing career. He bought a copy of *Weird Tales* and read a story, "Pickman's Model" written by H.P. Lovecraft. Impressed, Bloch sought out other Lovecraft stories but, when he discovered that the bulk of

Lovecraft's work was found only in *Weird Tales,* he wrote a letter to Lovecraft, and thus began a friendship that lasted for nearly a decade, existing only in letters. Lovecraft lived in Providence, Rhode Island, and was too poor to do much traveling.

Ray Bloch was a banker and, when the Depression struck in October of 1929, he lost his job and the family moved to Milwaukee, eventually living at 620 East Knapp Street.

Lovecraft's influence continued, as Bloch later explained: "Quite early in our correspondence, HPL suggested that I might be interested in trying my own hand at writing with an eye to publication. A quick inventory of physical assets confirmed that I did indeed possess a hand and an eye, plus backups. And since Lovecraft's suggestions generously included his willingness to inspect my efforts, what more did I need?"

His writing soon paid off, thanks to Lovecraft's discerning eye, which always offered suggestions toward revision of the stories Bloch would send him before submitting to the magazines. In 1934, Bloch had his first short story published, "Lilies," by *Marvel Tales.* When he graduated from high school in Milwaukee, Bloch could see that the Depression was taking its toll and jobs were scarce. He decided to try writing full-time.

Both of Bloch's parents supported the idea, and so he went to work. He targeted *Weird Tales,* and in less than a month had an acceptance letter for "The Secret in the Tomb" — and a check for twenty dollars. Bloch quickly turned out another tale which was somewhat better and so the editor switched the tales around. "The Feast in the Abbey" became Bloch's first appearance in *Weird Tales.*

In 1935, Bloch got involved with a writing club, which he recalls with his usual sense of humor: "As far as I know, all the members of the Milwaukee Fictioneers were vampires," he later said. "They only came out at night."

Along with Raymond Palmer, Al Nelson, Roger Sherman Hoar (who wrote as Ralph Milne Farley) and Stanley Weinbaum, Bloch soon learned to shape his craft. Another member was Jim Kjelgaard.

**Robert Bloch, left, chats with James P. Roberts. Photo courtesy of James P. Roberts.**

Through Lovecraft, Bloch was introduced to another *Weird Tales* writer, one who lived just 120 miles away — August Derleth.  Derleth originally had dim hopes for Bloch's literary career, but there eventually flowered a friendship between the two that would result in Derleth publishing Bloch's first hardcover collection of stories via Arkham House.  Bloch visited Derleth in Sauk City in 1935, returning there in 1938 with Henry Kuttner and Harold Gauer.

By 1942, however, Bloch's writing wasn't paying the bills. He went to work for the Gustav Marx advertising agency. Bloch would spend his days writing advertising copy and his nights writing macabre stories.  He had met Marian Holcombe earlier and they married. In 1943, their daughter, Sally, was born.

In 1945, Bloch's first book was published. *The Opener of the Way* contained some 30 stories previously printed in the pulp magazines. Bloch received $600 in royalties. One of Bloch's best known stories from the 1940s was "Yours Truly, Jack the Ripper." The story was then dramatized on the radio on — of all places — the "Kate Smith Radio Hour."

Bloch's first novel, *The Scarf,* came out in 1947, but it was apparent that for Bloch, the success of Ernest Hemingway was a long way off. To Bloch, one of the benefits to being a genre writer was the opportunity to attend the sci-fi conventions that had sprung up across the country beginning in 1939. Bloch's first convention was in Los Angeles in 1946. Other attendees were A.E. Van Vogt, Leigh Brackett, Wilson (Bob) Tucker, and, Bloch later said, "a youthful fan-turned-pro, Ray Bradbury. I often wonder what became of him."

By 1953, Bloch had struggled through his wife's tuberculosis, the death of his parents, and the temporary decline of the Gustav Marx agency. The Blochs moved to Weyauwega and Bloch commuted to Milwaukee to work. In 1959, Bloch appeared in Detroit to hand out the Hugo Awards, science fiction's top prize. To his surprise, "That Hell-bound Train" by Robert Bloch was voted Best Short Story.

Soon afterward, another Bloch story appeared on the TV show "Alfred Hitchcock Presents," which leads us to a fateful shower scene...

Robert Bloch wrote *Psycho* toward the end of 1959. Bloch writes in *Once Around the Bloch* (St. Martin's, 1993): "Elsewhere... I have recounted the story of the grim case which shocked Wisconsin in 1957 and led me, the following year, to write a novel in which a seemingly normal and ordinary rural resident led a dual life as a psychotic murderer, unsuspected by his neighbors. I based my story on the situation rather than on any person, living or dead, involved in the Gein affair; indeed, I knew very little of the details concerning that case and virtually nothing about Gein himself at the time."

According to Bloch's account of Hitchcock's purchase of *Psycho,* Bloch received $6,250, Hitchcock got *Psycho* and the rest is history. The movie was a hit and so compelling that some people who saw it were afraid afterward to take a shower. Bloch responded that they were lucky he didn't kill off the victim on a toilet seat.

In 1960, Marian's deteriorating health was a factor in

Bloch's moving the family to Los Angeles. There he would remain for the rest of his life. More books came out, Bloch began writing scripts for TV and movies, but *Psycho* represented the pinnacle of his literary career.

Life in Los Angeles put a strain on Bloch's marriage and, in 1963, they were divorced. Soon after, Bloch met Eleanor Alexander, whom he subsequently married. During the 1960s, Bloch's stories could be seen on TV in "Thriller," more Hitchcock specials and "Star Trek."

At the 1975 World Fantasy Convention held in Providence, Rhode Island, Robert Bloch was given the first Life Achievement Award. Other awards followed, but Bloch realized that they were minor achievements.

He continued to write almost up to the day of his death of cancer on September 25, 1994. His final book was his autobiography, *Once Around the Bloch*.

I met Robert Bloch in October 1992 in St. Paul, Minnesota. We were attending Minn-Con, a small convention devoted to dark and fantastic literature. Bloch was very personable as we sat at a table and talked about H.P. Lovecraft and Bloch's own career.

### ROBERT BLOCH: SELECTED READING
• *Psycho.* 1959, Random House, New York. 224 pp.
• *The Early Fears.* 1994, Fedogan & Bremer, Minneapolis. 515 pp.
• *American Gothic.* 1974, Simon & Schuster, New York. 224 pp.
• *The Night of the Ripper.* 1984, Doubleday & Company, New York. 228 pp.
• *Lori.* 1989, Tor Books, New York. 282 pp.
• *Such Stuff as Screams Are Made Of.* 1979, Ballantine, New York. 289 pp.
• *Once Around the Bloch.* 1993, St. Martin's, New York, 416 pp.

# HAMLIN GARLAND

In the pre-Civil War period, Wisconsin saw a shift of its population from the areas around the cities of Milwaukee and Madison into the western parts of the state. Migrant farmers were ever in search of new and better land. To the coulee area around La Crosse came Richard Garland, fresh from a winter of logging in Wisconsin's North Woods. He met Isabel McClintock and married her and to them was born, on September 14, 1860, a boy they named Hamlin.

Hamlin Garland spent his early years on a farm near West Salem and from a young age he was thrust into the hard life of a pioneer farmer. His father, however, always kept seeking new lands. When Hamlin was 8, the Garlands — father Richard, mother Isabel, and sisters Harriet and Jessica — moved to a farm near Osage, Iowa. Both Harriet and Jessica died very young. Hamlin went to school in Iowa, graduating from the Cedar Valley Seminary in Osage in 1881. Shortly after, Richard Garland moved the family again, this time to Ordway, in the Dakota lands.

When he was twenty-four, Hamlin left for Boston where he struggled to make a living.

Garland's first book was *Main-Travelled Roads,* published by the Arena Publishing Company in 1891. The stories here are "grim fictional portrayals of lives bound to the soil."

A wife runs away from her hard farm life with a rich ex-beau. An actor comes home to help his bitter brother. A soldier returns from war to a run-down farm. A banker lends land to a homeless family only to change the terms of the mortgage once the farm has been improved.

*Main-Travelled Roads* met with a storm of protest from the very people Garland portrayed.

In 1894, *Crumbling Idols: Twelve Essays On Art* was published by the Chicago firm of Stone & Kimball. It was an important book in its day and is still enjoyable reading today. Here Garland introduces his concept of liveritism, a theory combining elements of realism and impressionism in art and literature.

The following year saw the publication of *Rose of Dutcher's Coolly.* This is one of Garland's best novels. Rose, a wild, carefree girl goes from a coulee farm to school in Madison and then to Chicago where she meets up with high society. It's not your usual romance, however, as Rose is very strong-willed and Garland shows an unusual insight into the feminine psyche. Rose becomes interested in a cynical, older man, Warren Mason, who is a reporter on a metropolitan newspaper. Garland brings up thought-provoking questions on the institution of marriage. Mason is clearly one of Garland's best characters.

*McClure's Magazine* had commissioned Garland to write a series of biographical articles on Ulysses S. Grant to be later published in book form. *Ulysses S. Grant: His Life and Character* remains even today one of the definitive accounts of Grant's life.

In 1899, Garland had moved to MacMillan and they brought out *Boy Life on the Prairie.* Aside from the "Middle Border" books, *Boy Life on the Prairie* is the book most clearly associated with Hamlin Garland. This very enjoyable book gives details of his early life on the Iowa farm. Scenes of working in the fields predominate with asides given over to nature, school, and home life.

When he was 38, Garland married Zulime Taft. Her brother Lorado Taft was a well-known sculptor. They began a routine of spending winters in New York City, making spring and fall visits to the homestead and spending summers in the High Country.

By this time Garland had ventured into writing novels set in the West: *The Trail of the Goldseekers, The Eagle's Heart* and *The Spirit of Sweetwater* all told of his love of the "high country."

*Her Mountain Lover* is of that genre. A cowboy named Jim Matteson is sent to London to find a buyer for a gold mine that he and his partner have discovered. Here, Garland has fun contrasting the earthy, honest Jim with the staid, conservative Londoners. However, he "gits along" with a young woman named Mary Brien and she helps him

**Hamlin Garland. Photo courtesy of Wisconsin Historical Society. (WHi-N1804)**

to find a buyer. In one chapter, Jim describes a visit to a "haunted" mesa.

Garland's book *The Captain of the Gray Horse Troop* (1901) highlighted his interest in the American Indian, and Garland was among the first writers to write from the Native American viewpoint. His long-standing friendship with President Theodore Roosevelt gave Garland a rare opportunity to affect U.S. government policies as he pressed for more humane treatment of Indians.

Other Western books soon followed — *Hesper, Money Magic* and *Cavanaugh* — but Garland also wrote of his interest in the occult. *The Shadow World* and *Tyranny of the Dark* are novels about people exploring the paranormal.

These later novels met with declining reviews and sales.

By 1912, Hamlin Garland was 52 years old and discouraged. He began again to turn back to his childhood, putting down his memories as well as those gleaned from his father (his mother died in 1899). It wasn't until 1917, however, that Garland managed to sell *A Son of the Middle Border* to MacMillan & Company. The book was an instant success, both critically and financially, its poignant, reminiscent first-person tone awakening echoes in thousands of readers.

A later book, *A Daughter of the Middle Border,* picks up where *Son* left off, chronicling his marriage to Zulime and their two daughters, Mary Isabel (1903) and Constance (1908). It won the Pulitzer Prize for biography, though ostensibly the prize should have been for *Son.*

In 1926 came the third installment, *Trail-Makers from the Middle Border,* which told the story of his father's youth. It also drew good reviews and sales. Also in 1916, Garland went to Madison, Wisconsin, to be awarded an honorary doctorate in letters from the University of Wisconsin. Two years later the fourth — and final — book of the Middle Border, *Back-Trailers,* appeared. It was a fitting swan-song to Garland's career, or so it seemed to the reviewers.

Garland was now 68 and, as he put it succinctly: "...however, next year is not under bond to fulfill any promise."

Garland had, since 1916, lived in New York, moving there from Chicago after his father's death. Now, in 1929, Garland again moved, this time to California where he and Zulime settled near Los Angeles.

In his final years, Garland returned repeatedly to his journals in preparing a series of autobiographical books that sketch his life from 1914 nearly up to the present (1937). In *Afternoon Neighbors, My Friendly Contemporaries* and *Companions on the Trail,* he recounts episodes and visits with his literary contemporaries. The best of these is *Roadside Meetings* (1930), which covers an earlier period, 1880 to 1900, and presents fascinating accounts of "Walt Whitman Old and Poor"; Garland's loaning of $15 to a young writer to get a manuscript out of hock (the writer was Stephen

Crane and the manuscript *The Red Badge of Courage);* "walking the beat" with New York Police Commissioner Theodore Roosevelt; and showing Conan Doyle how to throw a curve ball.

Now past 70, Garland again took interest in the occult and life after death. His book *Forty Years of Psychic Research* (1936) is filled with "conversations" from his former friends and colleagues: Henry B. Fuller, William Dean Howells, Conan Doyle and others. In the same vein came *The Mystery of the Buried Crosses,* which reads like a fictional mystery, but Garland — resolutely at first and later only mildly — attested to its authenticity.

Age catches up with everyone and Garland was no exception. His research into "the death question" is liberally sprinkled into his later volumes of reminiscences.

On March 1, 1940, Garland had a cerebral hemorrhage. He died four days later. He left behind some 30 books, a wealth of memories, and a reputation as Wisconsin's "pioneer" author.

### HAMLIN GARLAND: SELECTED READING

- *Main-Travelled Roads.* (1891)— 1923, Harper & Row.
- *Crumbling Idols: Twelve Essays on Art.* (1894) — 1960, Harvard University Press, Cambridge.
- *Rose of Dutcher's Coolly.* (1895) Stone & Kimball, Chicago.
- *Boy Life on the Prairie.* (1899) — 1959, Frederick Ungar Publishing, New York.
- *Her Mountain Lover.* (1901) The Century Co., New York.
- *The Captain of the Gray-Horse Troop.* (1901) — 1930, Harper & Brothers, New York.
- *The Tyranny of the Dark.* (1905) Harper & Brothers, London and New York.
- *A Son of the Middle Border.* (1917) — 1968, MacMillan, New York.
- *A Daughter of the Middle Border.* (1929) MacMillan, New York.
- *Trail-Makers of the Middle Border.* (1926) — 1971, Scholarly Press, St. Clair Shores, Michigan.

- *Roadside Meetings.* (1930) MacMillan, New York.
- *Hamlin Garland's Diaries,* edited by Donald Pizer. 1968. Huntington Library, San Marino, California.
- *Hamlin Garland: A Biography,* by Jean Holloway. 1960. University of Texas Press, Austin, Texas.

*NOTE: Hamlin Garland's homestead in West Salem, Wisconsin has been fully restored to the period in which he lived there. it is open from Memorial Day through Labor Day, Monday-Saturday and by appointment the rest of the year. For more information, call (608) 786-1675.*

# CLIFFORD SIMAK

Clifford Simak is known as science-fiction's pastoral poet. He was born on August 3, 1904, in the ridge country of Millville Township above the Wisconsin River. He was raised on his father's farm there and the stone house his father built still gazes over to Prairie du Chien. Simak was educated in Patch Grove and taught school for a few years in other small towns in the neighborhood. All that area in southwest Wisconsin became the country of his imagination, Simak Country, which to many is as real as the inventions of others.

After graduating from the University of Wisconsin in Madison, Simak moved to Minneapolis where he became a newspaperman. He wrote that newspaper work helped him develop a questioning mind and look beneath the surface.

Simak's first published story, "World of the Red Sun," appeared in 1931, in *Wonder Stories*. He then published nothing between 1932 and 1938 as the Depression set in and he was working for the *Minneapolis Tribune*. Most of Simak's best work didn't begin appearing until the 1950s.

Over the years, Clifford Simak wrote 27 novels and garnered every major science fiction award, winning Hugo Awards in 1959, 1964, and 1981; both the Hugo and the Nebula Award in 1980; and was awarded a Nebula Grand Master in 1976.

Probably Simak's best known work is *Way Station* (1963). In the shaded valleys of southwestern Wisconsin, Enoch Wallace, a survivor of the Civil War, lives a reclusive life in a farmhouse and with good reason: the year is 1964 and Enoch's longevity — he looks not much over 30 — has started to attract notice from outside. Gradually we learn that Enoch's farmhouse is a "way station" for space travellers from other galaxies. They arrive via an "intricate mass of machinery ...that wafted passengers through the space that stretched from star to star." Enoch has an alien friend,

**Clifford Simak, left, confers with Donald Wandrei, who founded Arkham House with August Derleth. Photo by Eric Carlson, courtesy of James P. Roberts.**

Ulysses, and is also friends with a deaf-mute neighboring farm girl named Lucy Fisher. Complications arise: the theft of an alien body, the threats by Lucy's rustic father, and a magical source of life called the Talisman.

Simak's pastoral style is revealed many times in this novel. *Way Station* is an absorbing read, echoing its magic all down the Wisconsin valley.

Another well-known book is *The Goblin Reservation* (1968). It's set on the campus of Time University, which is a thinly disguised futuristic University of Wisconsin in Madison. Several references to local landmarks show up in the story: the blue waters of Lake Mendota, the student union (Rathskeller), which in the book is 500 years old but occupies the same building; Bascom Hill (though it is not named); and a couple of local bars.

Peter Maxwell, a professor specializing in folklore and legends at the College of Supernatural Phenomena on the Wisconsin campus, returns from a trip through space via a transmitter that almost instantaneously transfers beings from one planet to another within the galaxy. Unbeknownst to him, his journey has been interrupted and he finds himself on a strange crystal planet. When he does return, he discovers that another Peter Maxwell has already returned and has been killed in an accident. Aided by his friends: Alley Oop, a Neanderthal who has become semi-civilized; Ghost, a spectral figure trying to discover just who he is the ghost of; and Carol Hampton, a pretty young woman with a pet sabre-toothed tiger, Peter Maxwell tries to unravel the mystery. He has also been charged by the inhabitants of the crystal planet to sell their storehouse of accumulated knowledge — knowledge gained over fifty billion years and two universes — in exchange for a huge block of an unknown substance called the Artifact that has been on Earth since before Man.

Part of Wisconsin has been turned into a reservation for other creatures of legend. Here, goblins, trolls, banshees, and fairies live together with little contact with humans. The O'Toole, a leader of the goblins, helps Peter Maxwell uncover a plot by another alien race called the Wheelers to buy the Artifact from the college for unnamed purposes. The Wheelers are a race physically composed of two large wheels and suspended between them is an eggsac containing hives of bugs who make up the intelligence of the Wheelers.

*The Goblin Reservation* is science fiction at its most enjoyable level. Simak plays with ideas, bouncing them into other angles and dimensions, leaving the reader with a sense of wonderment and the thrill of possibilities.

Clifford Simak's last story, "The Grotto of the Dancing Deer" about an immortal caveman who is the source of all the known cave art, won both the Hugo and Nebula awards in 1980.

Ill health plagued Simak in his final years and he died on April 25, 1988, yet he left a considerable legacy as one of Wisconsin's foremost science fiction writers.

## CLIFFORD SIMAK: SELECTED READING

- *Way Station.* 1963, Doubleday & Company, New York. 210 pp.
- *The Goblin Reservation.* 1968, Berkeley Medallion, New York. 192 pp.
- *The Best of Clifford Simak.* 1975, Sidgwick & Jackson (British edition) London. 252 pp.
- *The Civilisation Game.* 1997, Severn House, New York. 250 pp.

# GEORGE WILBUR PECK

He could have been the son of Tom Saywer and the grandfather of Dennis the Menace. He pulled off pranks that would stand with either of those two young hellions. He would influence the comic careers of Harold Lloyd and Laurel and Hardy. His real name was Hennery and he was created by a man who was to become both the mayor of Milwaukee and the governor of Wisconsin.

He was Peck's Bad Boy and his literary "father" was George Wilbur Peck, who founded the *Milwaukee Sun,* which boasted that it was "the funniest paper in America — what vaccination is to the small pox, Peck's *Sun* is to the Blues ."

George Peck was born in 1840 in Henderson, New York. In 1843, his family moved to Whitewater, Wisconsin, where Peck attended elementary and high school and where, no doubt, he received inspiration for many of the adventures of the Bad Boy.

When Peck was 15, he began his long career in the newspaper business by hiring out as an apprentice printer with the *Whitewater Register.* A year later he moved on to the *Jefferson County Republican,* where he worked until the start of the Civil War. In 1863, Peck enlisted in the Union Army. After the war, he moved up to Ripon to found his own newspaper, *The Representative,* where he began publishing a popular series of comic sketches involving an Irishman named Terence McGrant. These sketches led to Peck's move to New York to work for the *New York Democrat.* How many newspaper staffers boast the bipartisan distinction of working for both a Republican and a Democrat paper?

Peck's stay in New York was short, however, and 1871 found him in La Crosse, Wisconsin, where he published his first book, a collection of his sketches called *The Adventures of One Terence McGrant.* In 1874, Peck found his niche — Milwaukee, where he again founded a newspaper, *The*

*Sun,* in which he felt free to unleash his wacky humor upon an unsuspecting public.

By 1884, *The Sun* had a circulation of 80,000 and was sold on trains and newsstands all over America. Here, Peck began his most famous series of sketches, the ubiquitous Bad Boy whose over-the-top pranks were eagerly followed by millions of young boys eager to learn new deviltries.

Peck's Bad Boy sketches usually featured the Bad Boy entering a grocery shop, where he would recount to the grocer his latest prank. Most of the time, the Bad Boy's father was the dim-witted victim. While telling his tale, the Bad Boy would try to snitch food and afterward pull a prank on the grocer. The grocer had enough boy left in himself to appreciate these *bon-mots* and often tried to one-up the Bad Boy.

The first collection of the Bad Boy sketches appeared in 1883, *Peck's Bad Boy and His Pa.* As E.F. Bleiler states in his introduction to the 1958 Dover reprint: "Peck was obviously writing to suit the tastes of his time, and for his own pocketbook, not for posterity. And as a result his work contributes one of the better culture gauges for his time. He mirrors the hidden feelings of his time and place much better than many more serious and self-conscious books...

"Peck's mirroring of social forces, however, is equally important. He wrote in a transition era...between Victorian stability and modern change. He stood far enough from the past to be critical and ironic, yet close enough to ... poke fun at the most sacred institutions."

In Peck's Bad Boy, there are words that were part of the vernacular of the times but that would be considered offensive today, especially when we find *Tom Sawyer* and *Huckleberry Finn* being pulled off library shelves because of one particular word — which is also used by Peck's Bad Boy.

In *Peck's Bad Boy and His Pa,* many "sacred institutions" get their comeuppance. The local deacon and the preachers are victims, so are church choirs and the hoity-toity upper class. Pa is usually the unwitting distributor of these pranks and thus gets all of the blame. Ma finds herself the innocent victim, sometimes caught in the backlash, but she is also hypochondriacal and often takes to her bed. Later in the book, to the reader's amazement, Ma and Pa have a baby, which affords more grist for the practical joke mill. The Bad Boy has an unnamed "chum," his sometime partner in crime, who dresses up as a girl and tries to seduce Pa. All these are ingredients that keep *Peck's Bad Boy and His Pa* a fast-paced and entertaining read. Many Milwaukee places and surrounding areas are mentioned in the book — there are side trips to Wauwatosa, Racine and Pewaukee. Waupun is noted as a place where Bad Boys are sent.

George Wilbur Peck. Photo courtesy of Wisconsin Historical Society. (WHi-2651)

Other Bad Boy books followed: *The Grocery Man and Peck's Bad Boy,* also known as *Peck's Bad Boy No. 2* (1883), *Peck's Bad Boy Abroad* (1905), *The Adventures of Peck's Bad Boy* (1906), *Peck's Bad Boy with the Circus* (1906), and *Peck's Bad Boy with the Cowboys* (1908).

In *Peck's Bad Boy Abroad,* the premise is that Pa is in a bad way with various illnesses and decides the only way he is to get better is to travel all over the country and the world. The Bad Boy relates all this to his friend, the grocer, in the first chapter, and the rest of the book is in the form of letters from Hennery to the grocer. Some of the words in the story might baffle the modern reader: To get a "hot box" (a railroad term) is to get angry; "condemned" is "God damned," but of course, you couldn't print that then.

The Bad Boy and his Pa first go to Washington and meet with Teddy Roosevelt, then to England for a chat and a drinking bout with King Edward. Seasickness on the ocean voyage is described in stark but humorous terms. In Paris, Pa is buncoed by a pretty woman (it happens often) but they do go up the Eiffel Tower, which Pa calls the "Keeley cure" for dipsomaniacs. More adventures in Europe follow:

Monte Carlo, where they lose all their money gambling; Switzerland, where Pa falls off a "glazier;" and, finally, in Rome, where they are blessed by the pope — a futile gesture if there ever was one — and see dead bodies in the catacombs.

In Russia, the Bad Boy and his Pa inadvertently become part of a revolution. In one scene, the Cossacks fire on the crowd gathered in front of the Winter Palace. Pa goes on a wolf hunt "...in a piece of woods that looked quite wolfy." From Russia, it's on to Turkey, where Pa thinks the Turks are fellow Shriners from Chicago. The Sultan of Turkey passes by a crowd silent in hushed reverence. This is too much for the Bad Boy and his Pa, so they burst into song, and the song is a University of Wisconsin fight song.

Then it is on to Egypt. He describes the Egyptians in terms that today would be denounced as racially offensive, but in the context of the early twentieth century were intended as humor. Pa rides a camel and afterward is "lame from Genesis to Revelations." Other destinations follow, with pranks being committed all the way.

Aside from the Peck's Bad Boy series, George Wilbur Peck wrote books about his Irish friend, Phelen Geoghan, as well as *Uncle Ike and the Red-Headed Boy* and also *Wisconsin: Comprising Sketches of Counties, Towns, Events, Institutions, and Persons, Arranged in Cyclopedic Form,* which he edited for the Western Historical Association.

Not all of Peck's columns for the *Milwaukee Sun* were about the Bad Boy. He also wrote on topical themes and the best of these were collected in *Peck's Boss Book.* "Actresses Playing Love" compares two actresses, a novice and a professional, and uses baseball phrases as similes for what constitutes a proper lover. In "The Popularity of Boxing," the actions of the boxing ring are transplanted to Shakespearean tragedy, notably *Hamlet.*

Another sketch discovers Adam and Eve and the devil in the Garden, but they are affected by modern customs. "An Army on Strike" is about a Shakespearean play in Madison, which is endangered when the boys — all four of them — hired to play  soldiers rebel at the measly pay.

Not all of the sketches were humorous. "His Baby Was Dead" is a poignant account of a railroad conductor's tragedy. "The Female Husband" is an early story of lesbianism. "The Bicycle Convention" explores all the uses to which a bicycle could be put — from grocery deliveries to modern warfare. "A Pop Factory Wanted," a tirade against soda pop is very funny but short-sighted considering the status of Pepsi and Coca-Cola today.

"About the Upper Lip" describes the perils of shaving off a moustache, especially in romance. Peck's Boss Book contains 72 such articles and is entertaining reading even today.

George Peck was elected mayor of Milwaukee in 1890 and governor of Wisconsin in 1894, each time on the Democratic ticket. He was a popular politician, ready with a quick joke or a sharp rejoinder. After being defeated for a third term as governor, Peck retired from public life, except for occasional appearances as a dinner speaker.

Peck died in 1916 at the age of 76, but his legacy remains to this day, whenever anybody uses the phrase "Peck's Bad Boy."

### GEORGE WILBUR PECK: SELECTED READING

• *Peck's Bad Boy and his Pa,* Belford & Clarke, Chicago & New York, 1883. (Dover reprint edition, 1958.) 347 pp.

• *Peck's Bad Boy Abroad,* Thompson & Thomas, New York. 1905. 379 pp.

• *Peck's Boss Book,* Belford & Clarke, Chicago & New York. 1884, 252 pp.

# GEORGE VUKELICH

I had spent the 4th of July holiday in 1995 with friends and relatives in my hometown of Waterloo, Iowa. Upon returning to Madison the next day I opened the *Wisconsin State Journal* and saw the headline: "Noted Author, Radio Host Vukelich Dies At 67."

The shock was almost as great as when my own father died at the age of 58. For George Vukelich, through his writings and the few conversations we had, mostly at bookstore signings or when he was part of the August Derleth Society, had been almost like a second father. His words of wisdom in books like the two volumes of *North Country Notebook* were indeed paternal.

Very few writers were as in tune with the outdoors as George Vukelich. Even August Derleth seemed a bit remote from the nature he was observing and recording. George Vukelich lived in the outdoors. The great irony between the two men is that they died on the same day — July 4th.

George Vukelich was born in South Milwaukee on July 5, 1927, to Frank and Florence Vukelich. Despite the occasional glimpses of his boyhood that Vukelich reveals in his articles and essays, not much is known about his early life. He called his grandparents Baba Jula and Tata, and until he was 7 years old, his primary language was Romanian.

Several times Vukelich wrote of his days in school where he later created The Seven-Foot Nun who would dispense wisdom and the ruler with equal prowess. While still in his teens, Vukelich joined up with the merchant marine. These experiences helped to shape his social consciousness.

After the war, he enrolled in college and studied fiction writing under the tutelage of Mari Sandoz and August Derleth.

In 1962, Vukelich had his first novel published: *Fisherman's Beach.* The novel opens with Old Man La Mere, a Great Lakes fisherman who is bed-ridden. His health is failing, but he is cantankerous and seemingly indomitable.

His five sons range in age from Germaine, who is 35, to 11-year-old Reuben. La Mere is watched over by his over-solicitous wife and the doctor, Le Coutre. His only ally is the fat priest Father Doucette.

Germaine is an Army pilot stationed in Paris. The others, Roger and the twins Gabriel and Raphael, carry on in the family tradition of fishing.

A new bill is introduced in the state Legislature that would negatively affect the fishermen plying the boats and nets on the Great Lakes. La Mere is about to go to Madison to protest when he collapses with a heart attack.

Germaine is called home, bringing with him a surprise — his 5-year old daughter Julia. Vukelich often uses fishing metaphors to describe life situations.

Roger La Mere always had plans to take over the Old Man's fishing business. Germaine's arrival and his relationship with the Old Man now pose a threat. Germaine himself is very reluctant to mix in the family's affairs — having been away for six years, he feels an interloper.

Young Reuben is just starting to discover the boundaries between life and death. He receives a .22 caliber rifle and uses it to shoot a seagull which draws a life lesson from Papa La Mere. Germaine remembers his own lesson from the Old Man which involves a huge turtle found in the middle of the road when Germaine was seventeen.

Another factor complicating Germaine's return is Ginny Dussault. Years ago, they had a season of young love, but while Germaine went on with his life, Ginny had stayed in Two Rivers. Roger has been dating Ginny and while the brothers are out on the lake in the tug, Roger lets Germaine know the situation: he plans on marrying Ginny and inheriting Old Man Dussault's fishing business as well.

But the affairs of this family, as with most, don't follow one member's script.

The late 1960s saw Vukelich passionately involved in the anti-Vietnam War movement. He became a radio personality. His uniquely modulated voice was a natural for the medium. Playing soft jazz music, he was "Papa Hambone" who would tell stories between selections. Later,

Vukelich developed a show called "Pages From A North Country Notebook" in which he called our attention to current environmental issues.

Vukelich wrote articles for newspapers, but in 1977 workers at Madison Newspapers, which published both the *Wisconsin State Journal* and Madison *Capital Times,* went on strike. Vukelich took his place with the strikers and he never again saw his work published in either paper. But Vukelich never wavered from his stand. When the strike newspaper *The Madison Press Connection* began, Vukelich devoted his first column to an attack on his former co-workers who had crossed the picket line. The strike newspaper lasted two years and Vukelich moved on to join the weekly alternative newspaper, *Isthmus.* There, his *North Country Notebook* columns found a new and eager audience among young college students.

In 1987, Vukelich published a collection of his essays that had previously appeared in *Wisconsin Trails,* the Madison *Capital Times,* and *Isthmus. North Country Notebook* was published by his own North Country Press. Seventy-nine essays, such as one titled "The Loon," capture the spirit of George Vukelich and the outdoors.

"What The Crows Know" is a great short essay almost supernatural in effect. In "Send Me A Hawk" Vukelich goes out into the marsh to fish. He feels the presence of the Old Man (which he called his father) and August Derleth. In his mind George asks the Old Man to "send me a fish" and Derleth to "send me a hawk." The hawk appears. Later, as he is leaving the marsh, Vukelich notes: "You wanted a fish. You wanted a hawk. You did fifty percent this morning and a lot of people didn't do fifty percent. And they went to church." (p. 20)

Fishing is what Vukelich writes most about — all types and kinds of fishing, in all types and kinds of weather. Often, he describes natural forces in supernatural terms, as at the beginning of an essay titled "The Seven Foot Nun."

Not all of Vukelich's essays in *North Country Notebook* are of pristine wilderness and the joys of fishing. Although his "Alway's Up Murphy's Creek" begins humorously

**George Vukelich. Photo courtesy of *Wisconsin State Journal/Capital Times* newsroom library.**

enough, the tone quickly changes to anger at the pollution evident along the banks of Murphy's Creek.

Vukelich wrote well about hunting, too. His most regularly occurring character is Steady Eddy, who contributes pithy and telling comments, and these essays find Eddy in fine form. The section called "Hunting The Silence" deals with the intangible aspects of both the hunter and the hunted.

Vukelich's articles contain interesting and little-known tidbits of historical fact, such as in "Rock Island" which notes that the last survivor of the famed Boston Tea Party of 1773, David Kennison, lived on Rock Island when he was 110 years old and died in Chicago at the age of 116. "Little Brown Bats" is another gem of an essay. When you're cleaning fish in mosquito-infested country, brown bats can be your best friends, "It's like having Pappy Boyington and the Black Sheep Squadron, flying fighter cover overhead." (p.111)

The final section of *North Country Notebook* is devoted to those whom Vukelich treasured the most: his family. He also had something else in common with August Derleth: a respect for religion, but he often chose not to be in church. Both men preferred to be outdoors on Sunday mornings. "In God's greatest church," as Derleth often said, "the fields and meadows, the marsh and woods."

In 1988, Vukelich released an audio cassette tape of himself reading selections from *North Country Notebook*. Produced and engineered by Madison radio personality Rick Murphy, like Vukelich, a jazz enthusiast with his own late-night program at the time, this audio cassette lets the reader experience the sonorous and wry humor of Vukelich. "Shaman's Lake," "Snake Island," "Body Heat" and "Hibernating" are set to appropriate music and natural sounds which enhance the listening.

*North Country Notebook, Volume II* appeared in 1992. It opens with observations of the area near Aldo Leopold's famous "shack" up in the Baraboo Hills. Several of the essays were written since I had moved to Madison and I recall reading them in their original publication in *Isthmus,* a newspaper that allowed four-letter Anglo-Saxon words. When angry, Vukelich wasn't shy about using them. "Dark Side Of The Loon" is about the ugliness of the spear-fishing controversy between Ojibwe (Chippewa) Indians and the local whites in the Minocqua-Woodruff region of northern Wisconsin.

"Skinny-Dip" is a hilarious account of the young boy that

still resides in all grown men — even the good Father Himmelsbach. Whereas the first *North Country Notebook* took place outdoors, in *Volume Two,* there is a section called "The Legion Bar" and here is where you meet the good doctor, the good Father Himmelsbach and Gene the bartender — all the gang in Three Lakes, Wisconsin. They're all just sitting around the beer cooler discussing such highbrow topics as snoring, the best way to get through a North Country winter, and innovations in protective waders for those chilly trout streams. Too bad there weren't more Legion Bar stories.

Vukelich also recalls the great storms on the Great Lakes and what may be washed up on the beach the next morning.

The final section of *North Country Notebook, Volume Two* focuses on the Christmas season and contains one of my favorite Vukelich essays "The Spooky Spirit of Christmas.

George Vukelich died in 1995. Here is a poem I wrote to memorialize him:

*HUNTING GEORGE*
*—for George Vukelich (1927-1995)*

*I search in the still places*
*of the world*
*to find my friend, George.*
*This is where*
*he haunts us now*
*hidden in the secret niches*
*that tug at our conscience.*

*I hunt George in the still pages*
*of his books.*
*Seeing in the words:*
*woods, lakes, fish, birds,*
*the lonely hollows*
*Wisconsin has always held*
*sacred to his memory.*

*I talk to George there,*
*though I never see him.*
*But his voice comforts me,*
*the humor and wisdom*
*once again acts as a multi-*
*angled prism*
*that reflects the quiet glory*

*of a life well-lived*
*and a path to follow*
*until the grass claims flesh*
*and the loon calls*
*in the brilliant, never-ending night.*

## GEORGE VUKELICH: SELECTED READING

• *Fisherman's Beach.* 1962, St. Martin's Press, New York. (Reprinted in 1990, North Country Press, Madison, Wisconsin, 186 pp.)

• *North Country Notebook.* 1987. North Country Press, Madison, Wisconsin, 202 pp..

• *North Country Notebook, Volume Two.* 1992. North Country Press, Madison, Wisconsin, 130 pp.

• *Pages from a North Country Notebook.* (audio cassette) 1988. North Country Press, Madison, Wisconsin.

# JOHN MUIR

Anyone who drives north of Madison on Highway 51, continues through the town of Portage on Highway 33 to County Road F and then turns left and follows the road for some ten or eleven miles will see on the right side the entrance to a lovely little park and adjoining lake. A dirt road leads down to the shore of the lake and perhaps, if it is a bright and sunny morning, there may be a solitary boat bobbing gently on the placid waters and the figure of a fisherman outlined against the tree-lined opposite shore. Birds will be calling and perhaps a heron will be wading in the shallows. This lake and these few acres of surrounding land represent the origin of our National Park System as it is today. This is John Muir County Park and it was on these very acres and along this lake that "The Father of the Wilderness" as John Muir was often called, spent his boyhood and early adult years.

Though several sources do not list John Muir as a Wisconsin writer (for he rightly does belong to California), he lived in Wisconsin during his formative years and studied at the University of Wisconsin. Undoubtedly, his love of the land was born here, only to flourish in the mountains of California.

John Muir was born on April 21, 1838, near the town of Dunbar in Scotland close to the North Sea. In his youth, Muir often played games of derring-do with his brother Davey. When he was 11, Muir, along with his father, his brother David and his older sister Sarah, set sail for America.

Left behind were his mother, the oldest sister, Margaret, and the three youngest siblings who would join them later when the Muir family was settled.

The voyage took six weeks. A grain dealer in Buffalo, New York, convinced the elder Muir to travel to Wisconsin, and the Muirs settled on a farm near the town of Portage. Young John soon fell under the spell of the lush Wisconsin

**John Muir. Photo courtesy of Wisconsin Historical Society.**

countryside, so different from the bare rocky coast of Scotland. His observational habits extended to all types of animals, both domestic and wild. Of all the animal life around the Wisconsin farm, none so fascinated Muir as the myriad birds that sang in the woods and meadows.

Robins, brown thrushes, bobolinks, red-winged blackbirds, meadowlarks, orioles and tanagers all fell under Muir's watchful eye and appreciative ear.

The mystery of the loon, often heard but rarely seen, and the arrival each spring of the millions of passenger pigeons brought to young Muir an awareness of nature's beauty.

However, growing up on a Wisconsin farm left little time for these observations. Daniel Muir was a harsh taskmaster and a firm believer in the adage, "if you spare the rod, you will spoil the child." Beatings and whippings were delivered almost daily.

"If we failed in any part, however slight, we were whipped; for the grand, simple, all-suffering Scotch discovery had been made that there was a close connection between the skin and the memory, and that irritating the skin excited the memory to any required degree." *(The Story of My Boyhood and Youth)*

Seventeen hour work days were the norm, and even on Sundays there were chores to do before and after the church services. Young John was put to plowing the fields and digging a deep well for water. The digging almost cost him his life as one day he fell victim to "choke-damp," a poisonous gas that had gathered within the deep and narrow space of the well bore.

Muir also had a knack for inventing things. These were the precursors of the Rube Goldberg-like contraptions of a half-century later.

Muir created his own barometers, thermometers, and a truly strange device that combined the two as well as a hydrometer and a pyrometer. He took his inventions to the state fair in Madison and created a sensation with his clocks and thermometers. Meeting a businessman from Prairie du Chien, Muir accepted the man's job offer as a mechanical engineer and moved to the Mississippi River town, but after a few months he decided to return to Madison "to gain an education."

After an interview with the university president, Professor John W. Stirling, and because of the promise he showed with his inventions, Muir was readily accepted into the University of Wisconsin. Money still came hard to the young man (now 22) and when the summer vacation began, Muir walked the 35 miles from Madison to the Muir farm and spent the summer working at Fountain Lake, the farmstead now owned by his sister and her husband. Daniel Muir's religious fanaticism led to John's increasing estrangement from his father. Where Muir walked, there today stands a historical marker on the shoulder of Highway 51 to mark a favorite view of the Baraboo Hills where Muir would stop to rest on his long journey.

Muir tackled his studies in an amusing and systematic way:

"I invented a desk in which the books I had to study were arranged in order at the beginning of each term...Then, after the minutes allowed for dressing had elapsed, a click was heard and the first book to be studied was pushed up from a rack below the top of the desk, thrown open, and allowed to remain there the number of minutes required. Then the machinery closed the book and allowed it to drop back into its stall, then moved the rack forward and threw up the next in order, and so on, all the day being divided according to the times of recitation, and time required and allotted to each study." (*The Story of My Boyhood and Youth*, p. 139-140)

At the university, Muir studied chemistry, mathematics, physics, Greek and Latin, botany and geology. After four years at the University of Wisconsin, Muir left to go out and explore a greater university, that of the wilderness.

He walked to Canada and spent some time working in a broom factory. In March of 1866, the factory was destroyed in a fire, which also destroyed the notebooks that Muir had kept of his Canadian travels. Muir then went to Indianapolis, Indiana, and found work in another factory. While repairing a faulty belt, Muir lost his grip on a file and it flew up and pierced his right eye. Muir spent several weeks recovering and decided to "make and take one more grand sabbath day three years long" and spend his time studying nature. Thus began his "One-Thousand Mile Walk to the Gulf." He started the walk in Louisville, Kentucky, and walked all the way to the Gulf of Mexico. After spending five nights sleeping in the Bonaventure Cemetery in Savannah, Georgia, Muir contracted malaria, which didn't make its appearance until he had travelled to Cedar Keys, Florida. There, he spent months fighting the disease that almost killed him.

In March 1868, John Muir arrived in California. He took on several types of jobs until in late autumn he signed on as a shepherd for 1,800 sheep. The following spring, Muir returned to the Sierra Nevadas and began to explore the Yosemite Valley, which would become his home for virtually the rest of his life. In the book *My First Summer In The Sierras*, Muir accompanies a shepherd and his flock of 2,050 sheep as they move from the low pasture in the valley to the high summer pastures up around 8,000 feet. The shepherd, Billy, is a close-mouthed old coot who has been tending sheep for fifty years. He is content to watch the flock while Muir goes exploring.

Muir encounters a brown bear and "thought I should like to see his gait in running, so I made a sudden rush at

him, shouting and swinging my hat to frighten him." But
the bear stood its ground and Muir suddenly felt like he
might be the one running. After a long stare-down, the bear
casually turned around and ambled away. Earlier, Muir describes the shepherd's trousers: "...have become so adhe-
sive with mixed (bacon) fat and resin that pine needles,
thin flakes and fibres of bark, hair, mica scales, and minute
grains of quartz, hornblende....feathers, seed-wings, moth
and butterfly wings, legs and antennae of innumerable insects, or even whole insects such as small beetles, moths,
and mosquitoes, with flower petals, pollen dust...adhere
to them and are safely embedded, so that far from being a
naturalist he collects fragmentary specimens of everything
and becomes richer than he knows. His specimens are kept
passably fresh, too, by the purity of the air and the resiny
bituminous beds into which they are pressed."

In early August, Muir has a strange experience whereby
he "senses" the presence of a former mentor, Professor J.
D. Butler of the University of Wisconsin. When Muir left
Madison, Butler had said he would follow Muir's career and
visit him sometime. Indeed, a letter from Butler had arrived
in July — written two months earlier — saying that he
"might possibly visit California sometime this summer."
While Muir was sketching on the North Dome, he suddenly
"knew" that Butler was in the area. He rushed down the
mountain until he realized that he could not possibly get
to town before dark and thus had to wait until the following day. At the hotel, Muir learned that Butler had already
left to go climbing up the valley toward the Vernal and Nevada Falls. Using that strange Scottish sixth sense, Muir
found Butler easily and they spent a day and an evening
together. As Muir concluded with a wry humor: "Hawthorne,
I fancy, could weave one of his weird romances out of this
little telepathic episode, the one strange marvel of my life,
probably replacing my good old Professor by an attractive
woman."

Muir's stay in the Sierras lasted from the June 3 until
September 10. He always carried a notebook strapped to
his belt to record his observations. Thus, a description of

the moon: "I remember watching the harvest moon rising above the oak trees in Wisconsin apparently as big as a cart-wheel and not further than a half-mile distant. With these exceptions I might say I never before had seen the moon, and this night she seemed so full of life and so near, the effect was marvelously impressive and made me forget the Indians, the great black rocks above me, and the wild uproar of the winds and waters making their way down the huge jagged gorge."

And of a campfire:

"After the short twilight began to fade I kindled a sunny fire...Soon the night-wind began to flow from the snowy peaks overhead, at first only a gentle breathing, then gaining in strength, in less than an hour rumbled in massive volume something like a boisterous stream in a boulder-choked channel...My fire squirmed and struggled...detached masses of icy wind often fell like icebergs on top of it, scattering sparks and coals...the flames...roared as if trying to tell the storm stories of the trees they belonged to..."

In May 1871, Muir learned that Ralph Waldo Emerson was to visit the area. Muir tried to coax Emerson into spending a night camping out in the Sierras to fully observe and enjoy the bountiful nature that Emerson had always written about. "Of all people, I thought he would best interpret the sayings of these noble mountains and trees." But Muir's exhortations were not enough against the admonishments of Emerson's town-bound party who preferred the hotels to the outdoors. Muir went with them and watched Emerson's face in the light of the fireplace, the returned to his mountains.

Seventeen years later, Muir would travel East to visit Emerson's Concord, Massachusetts, and stand above his grave in the Sleepy Hollow Cemetery.

It was in 1871 that John Muir began the study that would soon bring him worldwide recognition. He travelled to the highest peaks of the Sierra Nevadas and studied the glaciers upon which he posited that the contours of the Yosemite Valley were caused by glaciation and not by an earthquake as was the popular theory at the time.

Muir was urged by two of his friends, Clinton Merriam (a New York congressman) and John Daniel Runkle (president of Massachusetts Institute of Technology) to publish the results of his studies. Between 1871 and 1879 Muir would spend the summer months in the Sierra Nevada mountains and the winter in town where he would busily write articles for magazines and newspapers like the *New York Tribune* and *The Overland Monthly,* for which he would be a regular contributor.

In 1879 he visited Alaska for the first time and relentlessly explored the glaciers. Upon his return from Alaska, on April 14, 1880, Muir married Louie Wanda Strentzel. The 42-year-old Muir then settled down into a comfortable civilized life. "No one of the rocks seems to call me now." Subsequent visits to the Yosemite left him feeling like an outsider. Muir did return to Alaska in the summer of 1880, but was back in California by October.

It wasn't until 1889 that Muir surfaced again with two articles published in *The Century Magazine* that proposed the creation of a national park in Yosemite. The articles led to Congress passing a bill in October that created a park larger than Muir himself had envisioned. Over the next several years, Muir lobbied ceaselessly for the protection of the wilderness.

In 1890, Muir returned to Alaska. Now 52 years old, still hale and robust, he climbed over the glaciers in the same way as ten years before.

But he had some narrow escapes: "To shorten the return journey I was tempted to glissade down what appeared to be a snow-filled ravine, which was very steep. All went well until I reached a bluish spot which proved to be ice, on which I lost control of myself and rolled into a gravel talus at the foot without a scratch. Just as I got up and was getting myself oriented, I heard a loud, fierce scream, uttered in an exulting diabolical tone of voice which startled me...Then suddenly two ravens came swooping from the sky...evidently hoping that I had been maimed and that they were going to have a feast. But as they stared at me, studying my condition, impatiently awaiting for bone-picking time, I saw what they were up to and shouted, 'Not yet, not yet!'" (*Travels in Alaska,* p. 252)

Along with J. Henry Senger, a professor at the University of California, Muir created the Sierra Club, dedicated to preserving the mountains. Muir was named president and he held the position the rest of his life. In 1894, Muir's first book, *The Mountains of California*, was published.

To John Muir, nothing was as spectacular as the sunrise or sunset over the mountains:

"Now came the solemn, silent evening. Long, blue, spiky shadows crept out across the snow-field, while a rosy glow, at first just scarce discernible, gradually deepened and suffused every mountain-top, flushing the glaciers and harsh crags above them. This was the alpenglow...At the touch of this divine light, the mountains seemed to kindle to a rapt, religious consciousness, and stood hushed and waiting like devout worshippers. Just before the alpenglow began to fade, two crimson clouds came streaming across the summit like wings of flame, rendering the sublime scene yet more impressive; then came darkness and the stars."

Much of Muir's final years was spent travelling around the world. He visited every continent and in every case felt much more at home in the wilderness than in the cities. Muir noted the vast potential of the Russian landscape and his journal entries convey his realization of the gap between the splendor he saw in the cities and the rugged poverty in the countryside.

Muir was often visited by others who shared his vision of a national park system, including President Theodore Roosevelt with whom Muir spent three days on a camping tour of the Yosemite Valley. Mark Twain and Rudyard Kipling also visited Muir in California. Muir's final years were also saddened by tragedy; his wife Louie died in 1906 and his daughter Helen contracted pneumonia which forced a temporary move to Arizona. Books continued to appear: *Our National Parks* (1901), *Stickeen* (1909: the story of the dog that accompanied Muir on his Alaskan trip of 1880), *My First Summer In The Sierra* (1911), *The Yosemite* (1912) and *The Story of My Boyhood and Youth* (1913).

For all of John Muir's efforts to preserve the wilderness, his final attempt ended in failure as Congress in 1913 voted to allow the building of a dam across Muir's beloved Hetch Hetchy Valley to provide water for the city of San Francisco. His health failing, Muir was at work on his final book, *Travels in Alaska,* when he contracted pneumonia on a visit to his daughter. Muir died on Christmas Eve, 1914, and was buried in the family plot on his ranch in Martinez, California. He was 76 years old.

"The greatest [snow] storms, however, are usually followed by a deep, peculiar silence, especially profound and solemn in the forests; and the noble trees stand hushed and motionless, as if under a spell, until the morning sunbeams begin to sift through their laden spires." ( *Our National Parks* )

In 1916, the University of Wisconsin honored Muir (having previously bestowed upon him an honorary doctorate degree in 1897) by unveiling a bronze bust of him on what would later become Muir Knoll on the campus. His ingenious time-clock is still on display at the State Historical Society in Madison.

It was Edwin Way Teale who seemed to sum up John Muir the best:

"He was by turn a scientist, a poet, a mystic, a philosopher, a humorist. Because he saw everything, mountains and streams and landscapes as evolving, unfinished, in the process of creation, there is a pervading sense of vitality in all he wrote. Even his records of scientific studies read like adventure stories."

### JOHN MUIR: SELECTED READING
* *The American Wilderness: In The Words of John Muir,* 1973, Country Beautiful, Waukesha, Wisconsin, 192 pp.
* *Gentle Wilderness: The Sierra Nevada,* 1964, The Sierra Club, San Francisco, 167 pp.
* *John Muir: Nature Writings,* 1997, Library of America, New York, 888 pp.
* *The Wilderness World of John Muir* by Edwin Way Teale, 1954, Cambridge University Press, Cambridge, Massachu-

setts, 332 pp.

   • *Travels in Alaska,* 1988, Sierra Club Books, San Francisco, 274 pp.

# MARGERY LATIMER

Margery Latimer's name first came to my attention while I was a guest reader at the annual festivities honoring Portage-born author Zona Gale. There seemed to be some mystery as to who or what Margery Latimer was.

She had evidently left a mark upon the literature of Wisconsin and the city of Portage that still resonates more than sixty-odd years after her tragic death. Was she a neurotic waif as some have thought? Or was she a stubborn, headstrong young woman who caused a scandal by marrying a black man and living a free lifestyle? Or was she a visionary who, had her life not been cut short, would have gone on to become Wisconsin's greatest writer?

After reading Margery Latimer's two novels, *This Is My Body* and *We Are Incredible,* and her collection of short stories, *Guardian Angel and Other Stories,* I believe that not only would she have been Wisconsin's greatest writer, but one of America's greatest writers as well.

Margery was born in Portage, Wisconsin, on February 6, 1899. Her father, Clark Latimer, was a traveling salesman and her mother, Laurie Bodine Latimer, was a beautiful and gentle woman who loved books and music. Early on, it was apparent that Margery was "special," with a sense of life that lifted her above her fellow children. When Zona Gale's stories of *Friendship Village* appeared, Margery decided to become a writer herself.

It was a short story of Latimer's, first published in the local newspaper when Latimer was only 18, that led to an invitation from Gale to visit her at her stately home beside the Baraboo River.

Latimer soon became Gale's protegé, identifying with Gale's calm and cultured lifestyle to a point of almost frightening intensity. This would later surface in Latimer's novel, *We Are Incredible* and her novelette, *Guardian Angel.*

Latimer went to Wooster College in Ohio, but returned after just one semester, later enrolling at the University of Wisconsin. However, taking classes just forty miles from her hometown seemed to depress Latimer, who felt she needed a larger canvas to paint her life. In May 1921, Latimer followed Gale to New York, where she enrolled in a playwriting course at Columbia University and there met Blanche Matthias, who would soon become Latimer's life-long friend and adviser. The copy of *We Are Incredible* in the Special Collections Department at the University of Wisconsin Memorial Library has Latimer's inscription to Blanche written inside.

Latimer's sojourn in New York lasted less than a year. She returned to Portage and re-enrolled at the University of Wisconsin, where her writing now began to attract notice. She became part of a group of fellow writers, among them Horace Gregory, Carl Rakosi, Marya Zaturenska and Kenneth Fearing. Latimer gradually developed a romance with Kenneth Fearing, who was becoming well-known as a poet of the Edwin Arlington Robinson school. Latimer's parents, and also Zona Gale, voiced their doubts about Fearing. In part to continue her writing career and in part to break off the romance with Fearing, Latimer was persuaded to attend an artist's colony in upstate New York. Later, she would move to New York City where she stayed at the Old Chelsea Hotel.

Here, Latimer seemed to find her niche. Many of her Wisconsin fellows made the Chelsea a gathering place. Fearing arrived in New York and resumed their relationship. However, it became evident that he had changed. In *This Is My Body,* she describes a character based on Fearing as "dark" with a "dead mind" who jokes about important things. During this period, Latimer supported Fearing so he could write.

She moved in with Fearing and a friend of his, Leslie Rivers, but after a few weeks she had grown tired of cooking for and cleaning up after two men who were notorious for their bohemian lifestyles. Latimer wanted stability and time to concentrate on her writing. She had sold four sto-

**Margery Latimer and Jean Toomer. Photo courtesy of Joy Castro.**

ries and was still working on her novel, but she felt stagnant and adrift.

In early 1928, Latimer broke off her relationship with Fearing and returned to Portage. However, things were vastly different now. Zona Gale had met a long-ago friend, a much older man named William Breese, now a widower, and they fell in love. Latimer may have believed she was returning to her mentor, and was devastated that she didn't learn of the marriage until the night before the wedding. Unable to cope with even the commonplace events of daily life, she instead threw herself and her soul into her writing. The publication of *We Are Incredible* in October 1928, with its damning portrayal of a character clearly based on Zona Gale, led to a further distance between the two women, something that would only be resolved in the last year of Latimer's life.

Latimer followed up *We Are Incredible* with the publication in 1929 of *Nellie Bloom and Other Stories,* which received almost universal praise, elevating Latimer to the stature of contemporaries Katherine Mansfield and Elizabeth Moon. Still in the grip of her Muse, or Daemon, Latimer wrote a heartfelt justification of her life in *This Is My Body,* published in 1930. The book did not go over well with the critics. Stung, she returned to Gale's perceived betrayal by presenting an even more soul-destroying portrait in *Guardian Angel,* which was chosen as a finalist in the Scribner's $5,000 short-story contest. But by the time the story was published in June 1931, Latimer had met Jean Toomer.

Jean Toomer, author of *Cane,* a prose-poem about Southern Negro life that made his reputation overnight, was thirty-six years old and a classic Renaissance man. He was athletic, a dancer and a proficient musician. He had been a student at the University of Wisconsin for a semester several years before Latimer arrived there. He was all Latimer could ever have hoped to find in a man and she fell in love at their first meeting.

Toomer also was a follower of the Russian mystic Georg Gurdjieff and at the time of his meeting with Latimer, had assembled a devoted following of fellow Gurdjieffians in Chicago. Gurdjieff was a Russian who fled the country after the revolution and later founded the Institute for the Harmonious Development of Man in France that drew many students from America.

Toomer had been casting about for a place to establish a permanent community where they could practice the doctrines and disciplines espoused by Gurdjieff. Latimer suggested a place near Portage called Bonnie Oaks. It soon became notorious as "the Portage Experiment," seen much as John Humphrey Noyes' Oneida Community, which caused a scandal in the 1840s. Latimer soon became disillusioned with the concept and fled back to Portage.

Jean followed her the next morning, persuading her to return. They had become engaged.

Latimer and Jean Toomer were married on October 30, 1931. After the wedding, the Toomers went to Chicago, then on to New Mexico. Latimer began a novel based on what had transpired during the Portage Experiment. Latimer's stay in the West was the happiest time of her life. She and Jean learned that Latimer was pregnant. At this time, Latimer also reconciled with Zona Gale, staying in a house in San Diego that Zona had leased and meeting with Zona's adopted daughter Leslyn and the child's governess, Evelyn Hood.

From San Diego, the Toomers went up the coast to San Francisco and spent a few weeks with the Carmel art colony, making friends with Lincoln Steffens, Robinson Jeffers, Edward Weston and others. While in Carmel, Jean Toomer granted an interview to a local reporter about the Portage Experiment. A yellow journalist saw the interview and wrote a scathing article, accusing the Toomers of "mongrelising the white race." Scandal erupted, forcing Jean and Latimer into a state of siege in Carmel, not risking the outrage of people back in Portage. It wasn't until June 1932 that they felt safe enough to return to Portage at first, and then to Chicago. Latimer's child was due in August. She wrote to Zona that "it seems like my one supreme date with reality."

It was not to be. Latimer developed severe complications during childbirth. She remained conscious long enough to learn that she had delivered a healthy baby girl, then slipped into a coma. She died on Aug. 16, 1932.

Latimer's use of language is raw and vibrant. In the story "Nellie Bloom," Nellie goes to church on Easter Sunday: "She hurried into the church and, when they stood up to sing, music came out of her as if she were rising from the dead and from her feet she felt herself rise and, although she knew her body had not changed, it seemed to her that her flesh, her hips, her shoulders were pushing up, up, and she was all alive like something growing." Nellie's horrified awareness that a newborn has been placed in her lap is an unforgettable image.

In *This Is My Body,* Megan Foster attends the university: "I have to find everything in myself" is her credo. A friend asks her: "Which would you rather be? A great writer or a moral woman?"

Megan responds: "A great writer." She leaves college and goes to New York "where I can find reality." What reality? "The one everybody means."

"But you will suffer so much."

"I want to suffer," Megan replies. "I want to know."

Megan sees a poet from the university, Ronald, and falls in love with him. The next morning Megan feels "that all her flesh was a bright snapping liquid moving incredibly fast." Later, as Ronald leaves her and she withdraws "as if she protected herself with snake-sheaths of fear and all the dark clothing of inward-looking eyes."

The next chapter, "Walpurgis Night" is one of the grimmest things I've ever read, on a par with Sartre, Kafka, Beckett or Nathanael West. Ronald and Megan suffer trying to live in New York. Their arty friends are sycophants, whores and thieves. Megan's old friend from the university, Arvia Scott, arrives and reveals that she was forced into an abortion after having been made pregnant by Dean Sinclair, the head of the university.

Megan, too, has an abortion, but afterward she revolts against what she has done. She leaves Ronald and the last sight we have of her is Megan walking among the crowd with no home to go to.

*We Are Incredible* is Latimer's best work. It is told through three people: Stephen Mitchell, Dora Weck and Hester Linden. Stephen is aware of Hester's influence over the coterie of young people who gather at Hester's house: "Hester, he thought, liked to take healthy men and cripple them, make them her slaves and then turn them out. If they stayed around there would be minor irritations and she would gradually lose her hold, but if she sent them off herself she could hold them for good, providing they were fools like himself."

Dora Weck has just left Hester and she falls in love with Stephen Mitchell, despite his outwardly cynical demeanor. Once, Dora shouts at him, "I love you!" to which he coldly replies, "There is no such thing." Later, however, he is also torn between Dora's affection and the hold that Hester Linden still has over them both. "It isn't a trick... a trick couldn't make me feel as if my body was utterly yours," he tells Dora. At the end of the chapter, the telephone rings as Dora lies in Stephen's arms. It is Hester Linden, and Dora returns to Hester's house.

The final scene is focused on Hester herself and here we finally get a glimpse of the mysterious figure that has hovered like a shadow throughout the book. Hester is a very strange woman, always thinking, always attempting to control her feelings as well as those of the people around her.

Professor Joy Castro of Wabash College in Crawfordsville, Indiana, believes Latimer has been overlooked as part of a literary circle of modernists that included Ernest Hemingway, William Faulkner, James Joyce and Gertrude Stein. Through her writings and web site, Castro has tried to increase Latimer's visibility. Castro describes Latimer as one of the most powerful American writers of the 1920s and 1930s.

Even in death, Latimer herself became a mystery when an attempt was made to find her grave. She is buried in the cemetery in Portage, only a few dozen yards from Zona Gale's grave. Over the years, the cemetery has grown until the chart which located the plots was hopelessly out-of-date. Today, few people visit Latimer's grave and her books are scarce. A copy of *We Are Incredible,* when one can be found, is selling for $280. One can only wonder at what Latimer would have produced had death not snatched her just as she was finding her true voice.

### MARGERY LATIMER: SELECTED READING
• *We Are Incredible,* J. H. Sears & Company, New York, 1928. 283 pp.
• *This is My Body,* Jonathan Cape-Harrison Smith, New York, 1930. 351 pp.
• *Guardian Angel and Other Stories,* The Feminist Press, Old Westbury, New York, 1984. 246 pp.

# WILLIAM ELLERY LEONARD

Dusk was settling over Madison. The sun had disappeared below the horizon to the west and the skies above Lake Mendota, swept with archipelagoes of wind-riven clouds, shone a burnished orange. In their rented hotel room near the University of Wisconsin campus, Sherlock Holmes and Dr. Watson, on holiday from England, perused the newspaper and made plans for the evening. Holmes is standing beside the window, gazing at the street below when his attention sharpens. "Watson! Come here old fellow and tell me what you make of that chap?"

They view the singular scene. A man of middle-age, with a shock of white hair, wearing wire-rim glasses and a purple tie, has been walking up and down the street opposite where there is a public park that backs up to the university grounds. He makes as if to cross the street, then abruptly reverses himself and continues his walk back and forth, yet ever and anon his steps approach again the edge of the street. Through their open window there suddenly comes the sound of a locomotive whistle. The man below whirls around with a cry and now rapidly walks back through the park and disappears behind one of the university's buildings.

"Whatever was that all about, Holmes?" Watson asked, shaken. "Why the man seemed a veritable nervous wreck!"

Holmes tugged at the brim of his deerstalker and made to adjust his Inverness cape. "That, my dear Watson, was Professor William Ellery Leonard of the University of Wisconsin's Department of English. A brave man whose case is a classic of psychological phobias. And, alas, not even I can be of much assistance to him these days."

And thus begins the strange case of William Ellery Leonard, a man of wide learning whose chief claim to the literature of Wisconsin lay in just two books, *Two Lives* and *The Locomotive-God,* both autobiographical in nature which recount his first wife's suicide and the phobias that plagued his life from an early age, although their true source was not discovered until much later.

Jim Stephens, in *The Journey Home: Wisconsin Literature Through Four Centuries* (1989, North Country Press), likens the events in *The Locomotive-God* to "the feeling of *The Fall of the House of Usher* brought to life."

Born in 1876 in Plainfield, New Jersey, and named after Dr. William Ellery Channing, a Unitarian minister and Transcendentalist, Leonard can remember an incident that happened when he was 2 years, 4 months and 8 days old. Standing on the depot platform, he watches the arrival of the old steam locomotive which, to his mind, suddenly becomes a vengeful and all-powerful God. The terror of the moment shapes his life for the next fifty years, although the incident was soon buried in the subconscious: "On the contrary, trains became a childish passion and God a more than ordinary childish speculation."

Leonard's parents were stable and productive citizens. His mother established one of the first kindergartens in America and was fond of the Montessori method in teaching. Some of her own methods were peculiar. He was taught to read when he was 8 by a phonics system of sounding out the syllables. He wrote that he learned to read in a week or less.

When he was 8, Leonard also saw a cat maimed by the wheels of a switch-engine, thus building further evidence for the Locomotive-God in his subconscious.

He began school in the third grade. Two weeks later, there occurs another traumatic incident that leads to him being chased by a mob of young boys, jeering at him. The incident resulted in Leonard being transferred to a new school.

Despite his phobias, Leonard was an active youth: swimming, hiking, playing the usual children's games. He even was the catcher for the boy's baseball team. He learned to box and would no longer submit to the bullying by other boys of earlier years.

When he was 16, the Leonard family moved from Plainfield, New Jersey to a rural area near Bolton, Massachusetts (not far from Emerson's Concord). Being so isolated, he resolved to study at home, drawing up a detailed list of subjects and the times to study them:

5:30 - 7:30 Geometry
8 - 10 Greek (Anabasis)
10 - 12 Latin (Cicero)
12:30 - 12:45 Physiology
1 - 6 Work (Manual)
7 - 8 Latin Prose Composition
8 - 9 Greek Prose Composition
9 - 9:30 Physics
9:30 Retire

Manual work usually consisted of yard work around the house.

On a trip to Boston, Leonard mistakenly entered the offices of the College of Liberal Arts of Boston University. He was taken to see the dean who, upon hearing the story of Leonard's education, promptly enrolled him as a college student. Leonard stayed there four years and was accepted at Harvard.

At Harvard, Leonard was totally absorbed in his studies; his only companion was psychologist-philosopher William James.

Upon graduating from Harvard, Leonard went to Europe where, after visiting England, he spent a year in Germany. He returned to the U.S. and lived in Philadelphia for a time working on a dictionary which led to bouts of psychosomatic eye pain. He also took short-lived teaching jobs.

Finally, Leonard landed a teacher's post at the University of Wisconsin. He arrived in September 1906, at the age of 30. He found lodging near the university with a well-known and respected professor, the father of a friend he had met in Germany. Leonard fell in love with the professor's daughter. In his writing, he later called the professor Greylock and the daughter Agatha. In real life, they were

**William Ellery Leonard. Photo courtesy of Wisconsin Historical Society. (WHi-2656)**

John Charles Freeman and his daughter, Charlotte.

Leonard and Charlotte were married in 1909. Two years later, his wife, who had a history of depression, killed herself by taking poison. Leonard was publicly shunned and made the target of vicious rumors. Leonard's phobias soon developed in other ways. Always a good swimmer, Leonard now feared the water — not because of a fear of drowning, but because of the difficulty getting back to shore.

The most compelling part of *The Locomotive-God* is the description of the penultimate phobic attack which occurs in 1911. Leonard and Charles Brown (a pre-eminent archaeologist) take a walk seven miles from the university to the west side of Lake Mendota to look for arrowheads. They stop at a bar for a drink and Leonard lights a cigar at the same moment a train is passing by, blowing its whistle on the far side of the lake. This is virtually the same set of circumstances that created the original episode in 1878. Leonard and Brown reach the spot, but Leonard walks on to the shore of the lake. There, he sees another locomotive passing, and this time the Locomotive-God returns in full force. Leonard crumbles under the strain and, with Brown's help, rushes back to his house.

In 1912, Leonard published his first volume of poems, *The Vaunt of Man,* and dedicated it to his late wife. It is notable primarily for the ode to Abraham Lincoln, which was read upon the unveiling of the Lincoln statue that currently sits in front of Bascom Hall. The following year, Leonard began work on the autobiographical series of poems chronicling the tragic affair, *Two Lives.* Though *Two Lives* was written in 1913, it did not see print until 1922 because of the effect it may have created among those still living involved in Charlotte's suicide.

To his own surprise, Leonard got married again in 1914 to Charlotte Charlton. Their marriage lasted nearly twenty years, but Charlotte was soon caught up in the restrictions of Leonard's phobia. Yet, there was a brief time when the phobia lessened, and Leonard actually visited New York City, though most of his out-of-town excursions were limited to the Devil's Lake area — forty miles northwest of Madison.

It was on an excursion to Parfrey's Glen that the Locomotive-God struck for the final time. And in the twelve years from the time of that episode to the publication of *The Locomotive-God*, William Ellery Leonard's world was a half-mile area around the University of Wisconsin campus.

Leonard later married for a third time, to a graduate student nearly thirty years his junior, but that didn't last long. He later re-married his second wife and they stayed together until his death in 1944. His phobias did not prevent him from continuing to write and he published several books of literary thought, notably a translation of *Beowulf* and

Lucretius' *De Rerum Natura* (The Nature of Things). *A Son of Earth,* published in 1928, collected many of his earlier poems as well as selections from *Two Lives.*

William Ellery Leonard's poetry is considered out-of-date today. His work is classical in style and, save for certain lines of marked brilliancy, is easily passed over. A volume published posthumously, *A Man Against Time*, contains a few good high points.

### WILLIAM ELLERY LEONARD: SELECTED READING

- *Red Bird: A Drama of Wisconsin History in Four Acts,* 1923, B.W. Huebsch, Inc., New York. 150 pp.
- *Two Lives,* 1925, B.W. Huebsch, Inc., New York. 109 pp.
- *The Locomotive-God,* 1928, Chapman & Hall, London. 434 pp.
- *A Son of Earth,* 1928, Viking Press, New York. 225 pp.
- *Man Against Time: An Heroic Dream,* Appleton-Century, New York & London, 1945. 80 pp.
- *The Monster at the Center: William Ellery Leonard's struggle to stave off madness through art*, John Stark, Wisconsin Academy Review, Vol. 25, No. 1, pp. 12-17.

# MARYA ZATURENSKA

Marya Zaturenska is little-remembered today. If one glances at the list of Pulitzer Prize award winners in the category of poetry, one notices a mix of well-known names with those like her who have long been forgotten, names such as Leonora Speyer, George Dillon, Audrey Wurdemann, and Leonard Bacon. Marya Zaturenska deserves a much better fate than being primarily known as the wife of poet Horace Gregory.

Born in 1902 in Kiev, Zaturenska emigrated to the United States with her parents at the age of 8. The family lived in New York City in a house on Henry Street, which was near the Settlement House where other immigrants often gathered. While working in factories during the day, she attended high school at night.

In 1922, she received a scholarship to Valparaiso University in Indiana, but, a year later, upon the recommendation of Harriet Monroe, the editor and publisher of *Poetry* magazine, she transferred to the University of Wisconsin. She graduated from the Wisconsin Library School in 1925 and later that year was married to Horace Gregory. By this time her poems were already being published, notably in *Poetry* magazine which honored her with its Shelley and John Reed prizes for poetry.

Her first book, *Threshold and Hearth*, was published in 1934. Zaturenska's unique gift of language was already apparent. Her poem, "All Soul's Eve" immediately captures the imagination with lines such as:

"And through the doors there seemed to cling/A pale, dark aura wild and thin."

Her two autumn poems abound in rich imagery. "Prepare, O Death, to hold your last carouse" and from "Another Autumn" we find that "the hot earth breathes quietly again."

Many images have faded with time, or are replaced by

others. Who today knows that Death, usually represented by the cloaked, spectral figure with the scythe, was also represented by the spindle and the cypress tree?

Zaturenska features Death in many forms, as in "The Uninvited Guest."

*Cold Morning Sky* followed in 1937 and was selected from among the finalists for the 1938 Pulitzer Prize for Poetry award. In *Cold Morning Sky*, Zaturenska shows that her poetry had matured greatly in three years. She shows a wonderfully dark vision, full of winding stairways and even, at times, a pure mysticism. "The Lunar Tides" is one of Zaturen-ska's most powerful poems. Its language speaks to the dark night where "the vampire moon with yellow streams of light/Drains the dim waters, sucks the moist air dry." (p.12)

Throughout the book one comes across a particularly memorable turn of phrase, one that Zaturenska must have polished over and over again, such as "The sightless, impeccable Gods, who guard the sunsets" or, as in "The Emigres," the insertion of just one word transposes the entire meaning of an idea:

*In some forgotten paradise*
*fruitful and ripe and evergreen*
*Unserpented, serene.* (p.28)

The addition of "unserpented" reminds us of the Garden of Eden we have lost. In "The Dream," transcribed from an actual dream that Zaturenska writes of in a letter to the poet H.D. (Hilda Doolittle), she comes upon her own gravesite where "I saw the flowers, live roots among the dead" and "my tomb the smallest there," knows that life is fleeting and all is forgotten after death; which she characterizes in the very next poem: "Death, the dark serpent, heavy-eyed and holy."

In many of Zaturenska's poems the process of suffering often results in strength, the fortitude to endure, and even the knowing that one has endured.

Winter unveils its true meaning in "Legacy for Psyche" when "all seasons into snow dissolve." Even love must struggle through the harshest winter. One would be hard put to find a greater evocation of the Muse that drives us all than in the lines from "The Messenger."

"Season in Snow" is one of my favorite Zaturenska poems. A lovely, lyrical ode to the beauty of winter, though it also be a "chill and difficult world where loveliness/Divests herself of her rose-bordered dress." Life itself retreats inward toward contemplation and "men with muffled footsteps walking slow."

*The Listening Landscape* appeared in 1941. Mythology is woven into many of Zaturenska's poems. She sings of sirens and Ariadne's thread and the "Girl with the Golden Bough." Nature is often portrayed as an artist's canvas, as in "The Opening Book."

In "Landscape After Poussin," not all beauty is unreserved, "but antiquity's dream for younger eyes." The painting Zaturenska refers to is Poussin's Les Bergers d'Arcadie, which plays a part in one of the world's great mysteries, the location of the Holy Grail (cf. *The Encyclopedia of Unsolved Mysteries*, by Colin Wilson). "Forest of Arden" brings back the ghosts of World War I where the pastoral setting of today hides the horrors of what has taken place there. And there's an unforgettable image of a coffin brought forth in "Interview in Midsummer."

"The Casket of Pandora" is a brilliant poem, involving us in the consequences which abound and must be accepted with every action taken. Zaturenska continues with the mythological aspect in a poem that reflects the Medusa's point-of-view: Perseus as the deliverer of her abhorrent fate.

In "The Hostages" Zaturenska gladly gives her "hostages to fate" in the form of a "bright-haired eager son and vivid daughter."

"The Listening Landscape" is the city itself, all its myriad sounds and sights drawn into one sharp pattern, a living entity made up of disparate parts, like "In the suburbs women weep, and no hero comforts them."

Zaturenska rarely wrote about war, but when she did she again uses the structure of language to create a sense of uncertainty and dread.

*The Golden Mirror,* published in 1944 and dedicated to William Ellery Leonard, continued to reflect Zaturenska's themes: darkness mingled with beauty, nature and myth, and now that she was raising a family, love and children. In "The Tempest" the world is full of color, that intensifies when emotions give new and sharper images for the mind. "The Speaking Glass" is a mirror, but one that reveals truth, the truth of age and decay.

"Epitaph for a Careless Beauty" is a woman who has kept Love at arm's length until it was too late. Her beauty has faded and Love turns away.

"Death and Transfiguration" is a poem that should be included in any anthology of American poetry of the 20th Century. It is as memorable as Edna St. Vincent Millay or Emily Dickinson's meditations on death.

"Cathedral Town: Idyll and Prophecy" was written in Bath, England, during the summer of 1939. Zaturenska contrasts the peaceful quiet of this old town with the carnage that has again erupted in Germany, and she wonders how long the facade will last here, too, before all the walls crumble. "The Companion" is filled with the longing of the adult for the child, exuberant in the revealing of another of life's mysteries which the adult has taken for granted or entirely lost sight of: "My destiny approaches smaller than I have dreamed."

"Song for Christmas Eve 1938" is also somewhat prophetic, in a sense foreshadowing Hitler's invasion of Poland and the rise of Russia. The first stanza ends tranquilly, "sleep, hush, and holiday." But it grows progressively pessimistic, "the hope, the false daylight" from an eastern evening. "Peace" all the voices say, perhaps a reference to the British appeasement policies? But at the last we "see(s) the hidden figures hovering, poised to spring, poised to spring." (p.44)

"The Vision of Marie Bashkirtseff" is a haunting poem, a vision of her own death, reflecting on the glories of the past as her life flits before her eyes. At the end, she is the child again, lying in the coffin. In "The Recall of Eurydice" the mythological story is retold with beautiful imagery until she remains there [in Hades] now, "a nameless shade, amongst the nameless shades."

*Terraces of Light* was published in 1960 by Grove Press. It had been a long hiatus for Zaturenska, consumed by her devotion and caring of Horace Gregory and her children. She continued to write, however, and we see a continuing maturity in both her style and subject matter.

She writes of her childhood, a miserable and starving time in Russia, as a "Land of my childhood where/I never flowered or grew." Her vulnerability is revealed in poems like "The Waiting" when she asks "Who shields the sleeping tiger at my gate/And mocks me while I wait?"

"Virgin With A Lamp" speaks of women who escape from love which "...speaks through the air with the voice of a bird/Magnificent, and tragic, and absurd."

The fall of the Romanovs is eulogized in the brilliant poem "Four Ghosts" while "Girl in a Library" discovers love amidst the shelves of books, but the lover is the mystery of life. Memory continues to haunt her, as in "From a Winter Journal" Zaturenska calls out, "Blow your cold trumpets too, Memory/Mother of all the Muses answers you."

"The Dream Message" features "the eternal postman" who drops a thick letter into her hands. She anxiously rips it open, reads the words that signs her fate, then drops the letter to be consumed "in an internal fire." "The Mask" serves only to reveal the basic human personality underneath: "Beautiful mask, I know you now" is a quote from William Hazlitt. But what the mask truly lays bare is "That gilded skeleton that no one looked upon."

Marya Zaturenska's last book, *The Hidden Waterfall*, was published in 1974 by Vanguard Press in New York. She begins this collection with "A Shakespearean Cycle:" a series of poems written upon characters in William Shakespeare's plays. There is Prospero who "released from longing, sadness, shame" thus "I sail to exile once again;" Perdita, cast adrift, still seeking a home through the relentless storm; Cordelia, a lost woman seeking love, though it be of the darkest kind; Mariana, waiting for some unknown deliverer in her locked tower; Ophelia, sinking "through islands of dark water;" and Miranda, growing old, seeking in memory her "morning soul its early music render."

In "Another Snowstorm" Zaturenska recounts the years she has spent with Horace Gregory. A pagan mysticism hovers over "Chorale for the Seasons." Animals and spirits are one with Time, "it was your year of illusion." The poem is rather Chinese in its effect. Zaturenska's life-long love of Italy, both the land and its people, and enhanced by her earlier published biographical volume of the poet Christina Rossetti, are found here in a section called "An Italian Garland" which captures the flavor of five historical characters: Claudio Achillini, the famous Lorenzo de'Medici, the poet Torquato Tasso, Gaspara Stampa, and Vincenzo Monti. Memory also plays a part in "The Vision of Dido", a memory that can never be trusted because it "rose again, then flowed away/In the blind gaze that neither feels nor sees."

Both Marya Zaturenska and Horace Gregory died in 1982. They left two children, Patrick and Joanna, and several grandchildren. Recently, there has been a movement of reappraisal of Zaturenska. In 1996, an article by Mary Beth Hinton titled "Marya Zaturenska's Depression Diary, 1931-1932" was published in the Syracuse University Library Associates *Courier* and further excerpts from the diary covering the years 1933-1935 were published in 2001. An essay on Zaturenska appeared in the *Dictionary of Literary Biography* and Syracuse University Press published two books of her poetry..

Although Marya Zaturenska spent just a short time in Wisconsin, it was here, under the influence of Horace Gregory and other Wisconsin writers that she began her career as a poet — a career that in 1938 led to a Pulitzer Prize.

**NOTE:** *My thanks to Mary Beth Hinton of Syracuse University for sending me her articles on "Marya Zaturenska's Depression Diary 1931-1932" and "1933-1935".*

## MARYA ZATURENSKA: SELECTED READING

- *Cold Morning Sky.* 1937, MacMillan, New York. (reprinted 1970, Greenwood Press, Westport, CT. 62 pp.)
- *The Listening Landscape.* 1941, MacMillan, New York. 87 pp.
- *The Golden Mirror.* 1944, MacMillan, New York, 73 pp.
- *Terraces of Light.* 1960, Grove Press, New York, 78 pp.
- *Selected Poems.* 1965, Viking Press, New York, 210 pp.
- *The Hidden Waterfall.* 1974, Vanguard Press, New York, 69 pp.

# HORACE GREGORY

Horace Gregory, Marya Zaturenska's husband, had an extensive grounding in the classical poets of ancient Rome and Greece. His poems resound in allusions to these figures, both historic and mythological. They give to the modern reader a distinct sense of the age in which they were written, when Latin and Greek were commonly taught in the elementary and secondary schools.

Gregory was born on April 10, 1898, in Milwaukee. He was born into a fairly affluent family of businessmen and educators. Because he was sickly, young Horace never went to school until much later than usual. He was introduced at a young age to Greek and Roman mythology — first by seeing a statue of Atlas holding the sphere of the world on his broad shoulders and then reading Nathaniel Hawthorne's *Tanglewood Tales* given to him by his grandmother.

Gregory almost died from a burst appendix and the ensuing peritonitis when he was 7. It took him six months to recover. He spent his convalescent time reading. Early favorites were the Fireside Poets: Bryant, Whittier, and Longfellow, but Gregory soon graduated to weightier material: Shakespeare, Dickens, Keats and Byron. He found Whitman mostly boring. Living in Milwaukee and under the guidance of his Aunt Victoria, Gregory discovered the cultural treasures — as it were — of the Midwest; one of those being The Wisconsin Players who often brought poets up from Chicago to read. Gregory attended readings by Carl Sandburg, Vachel Lindsay and even Robert Frost.

Aunt Victoria found a young woman to come in and tutor Gregory. She was Grace Lusk, a former educator who had suffered a nervous breakdown and was staying with the Gregorys to recover. She tutored Horace well enough that he was later admitted to a school where boys prepared for college at Yale. Later, Lusk met a man who wanted help in writing a book. She left with him and a few months later was arrested and sent to prison for murdering her employer's wife in one of Wisconsin's most famous murder cases. Gregory visited Lusk in a sanatorium. She disappeared again after her release.

After a visit to New York, Gregory wanted to expand his horizons and go to a college in the East, but his family had fallen on hard times and couldn't afford it, so Horace settled for the University of Wisconsin in Madison. His frail health was always a concern.

Madison's liberalism also seemed to liberate Gregory. He enjoyed a new sense of personal freedom from all he had left behind in Milwaukee. Early on, he met William Ellery Leonard, author of a translation of Lucretius, *De Rerum Natura* .

Another influence on Gregory's college days was Latimer. Gregory spends several pages of his book *The House On Jefferson Street* on Latimer. When he left Wisconsin for New York after graduation, Latimer and Kenneth Fearing had already preceded him and they formed a little society that met in their apartment at the *Chelsea Rooming House,* which subsequently became the title of Gregory's first book of poetry.

Latimer's colorful, eccentric, and buoyant personality had a far-reaching effect on the shy Gregory. He also had a brief friendship with Stanley Weinbaum and it is interesting to note what Gregory had to say about writing science fiction: "...the plotting of a science fiction fantasy is often a colorful and intricate affair, one that delights the creator as well as his readers." Gregory's own excursions into science fiction were limited to H.G. Wells and Arthur C. Clarke.

After three-and-a-half years, Gregory left Madison for New York. In his first few months in New York, Gregory struggled to write poetry and earn a living at the same time. He got a few jobs writing book and movie reviews, but by November (he had left in February) of 1923, he was starving, alone, and finally a bout of jaundice brought his mother to New York to care for him. Gregory returned to Milwaukee briefly, but was soon back in New York where in the summer of 1925 he was introduced to "a slight, dark-haired, beautiful girl in a fluttering lilac-tinted organdy dress, who was as passionately devoted to poetry as I was." The girl was Marya Zaturenska, who had just returned to New York after graduating from the University of Wisconsin's Library School.

They soon married and set up shop in an apartment on Washington Square. Life in New York was never easy for the couple, who were soon joined by a son, Patrick, and a daughter, Joanna. Yet they accepted their poverty as a seemingly mandated accompaniment to their desire to write poetry. Marya's poems had already been published in *Poetry* magazine and she had befriended the editor, Harriet Monroe, while at the University of Wisconsin.

In 1926, after failing at a couple of ill-suited jobs, the Gregorys moved from Washington Square to Sunnyside, a low-income housing development. Their stay was marred by an influx of radical Communist supporters, whose inflammatory rhetoric was soon at odds with Horace and Marya's apolitical bent. With relief, they accepted an invitation to stay at Yaddo, a writer's community in upstate New York near Saratoga Springs.

*Chelsea Rooming House* was published by Covici-Friede in 1930, followed shortly after by Gregory's translation of the poems of Catullus. T.S. Eliot had also accepted it for publication in England under the Faber & Faber imprint, though under the title of *Rooming House* alone. Gregory went to hear Eliot read when Eliot visited New York and was enthralled by the poet.

In 1933, *No Retreat* was published. The year also brought an invitation to visit England from the poet "Bryher" (Winifred Ellerman). The Gregorys visited England and Ireland in 1933, and for Horace Gregory, the visit he made to Dublin's Trinity College completed a circle, for his great-grandfather had also attended Trinity.

In 1935, Horace Gregory began teaching at Sarah Lawrence College, where he remained on the faculty for more than 40 years. He continued to publish books of poetry and also critical studies of both contemporary and classical authors. His *Pilgrim of the Apocalypse* (1933) was one of the first important critical studies of D.H. Lawrence. A book published in 1944, *The Shield of Achilles : Essays on Beliefs in Poetry,* is an entertaining book filled with graceful and moderate commentary on nearly two-dozen literary figures: the well-known — Lord Byron, Edgar Allan Poe, Lewis Carroll, Wordsworth, Yeats, D.H. Lawrence; and the lesser-known — Walter Savage Landor, John Clare, Thomas Lovell Beddoes and William Ernest Henley. In his essay on Walter Savage Landor, Gregory compares the epic narrative poem to "many of the present experiments in radiodrama." Which prompts the question: Was this written before or after the infamous Orson Welles broadcast of H.G. Wells' "The War of the Worlds"?

He wrote biographies of Amy Lowell and James MacNeill Whistler and, with his wife, compiled several anthologies, including *A History of American Poetry 1900-1940.* His classical translations include the poems of Ovid and Catullus, and also Ovid's *The Metamorphoses.*

Horace Gregory's long life came to a close on March 11, 1982, at his home in Shelburne Falls, Massachusetts.

Much of Horace Gregory's work merits closer attention, from the simplistic poetry of *Chelsea Rooming House,* written during the height of the Depression (many poems here express this sense of futility); to the experimental forms of several long poems set as short plays in the 1961 collection *Medusa In Gramercy Park.*

In this collection we also have the beautiful "A Wreath For Margery," Gregory's ode to Latimer. *Chorus For Survival,* published in 1935, offers the grim scene of the New York subway.

A later poem, "Police Sargeant Malone and the Six Dead Drinkers," contains an echo eerily reminiscent of a famous quotation by one of the characters in Fyodor Doestoyevski's novel *The Devils* who said that, rather than die at once, he'd prefer to stand for all eternity on a narrow ledge above an abyss. After a long hiatus, Gregory published his final volume of poetry in 1976. It is full of the quiet wisdom one often sees in old age. The poem "The Moonlight Curtains Stir at Three O'Clock" is a serene elegy.

### HORACE GREGORY: SELECTED READING

• *Chelsea Rooming House.* 1930, Covici-Friede Publishers, New York. 65 pp. Also published in England as *Rooming House,* 1932 Faber & Faber, London 48. pp. The American edition has 3 extra poems.

• *No Retreat.* 1933, Harcourt, Brace Publishers, New York. 51 pp.

• *The Shield of Achilles: Essays on Beliefs in Poetry.* 1944, Harcourt Brace & Company, New York. 211 pp.

• *Medusa in Gramercy Park.* 1961, MacMillan, New York. 65 pp.

• *The House on Jefferson Street.* 1971, Holt, Rinehart, and Winston, New York. 267 pp.

• *Collected Poems.* 1973, Holt, Rinehart, and Winston, New York. 225 pp.

• *Another Look.* 1976, Holt, Rinehart, and Winston, New York. 55 pp.

# GLENWAY WESCOTT

Glenway Wescott was born on April 11, 1901, in Washington County near Kewaskum, Wisconsin. He was the oldest of six children. His father raised pigs on the family farm, a hundred acres of mostly poor soil. Glenway soon proved himself "too sensitive" for such work. He spent most of his childhood reading "shocking material" in Leviticus and Deuteronomy and by the time he was 13 he had begun to write stories and essays, which appeared in his West Bend High School literary publications.

When Wescott entered the University of Chicago at age 16, he soon found himself in congenial company, where he flourished. Along with the poet and critic Yvor Winters and novelist Elizabeth Ford Roberts, the university's Poetry Club (of which Wescott quickly became president) also hosted Vachel Lindsay, Carl Sandburg and Edgar Lee Masters, among others. It was also at this time that Wescott met Monroe Wheeler, a bright and ambitious young man who would soon become Wescott's lifelong companion. Wescott's poetry began appearing in magazines, *Poetry* and *The Dial,* and he spent his early twenties travelling and living for periods in New York, England, and Germany.

Wescott settled in New York and he worked on his first novel, *The Apple of the Eye,* which was published by Dial Press in 1924. The story of Wescott's childhood life on the farm, it showed that Wescott had a flair for the nuances of language and skill at showing the relationships within a family circle. In early 1925, Wescott and Monroe Wheeler went to Paris but soon moved south to Villefranche, near Nice. He became one of the American expatriates living in France. He met Ernest Hemingway, who disliked Wescott's gay lifestyle and portrayed Wescott as "Roger Prentiss" in *The Sun Also Rises.*

*The Grandmothers* was published in 1927 and launched Wescott to fame. It won the Harper Prize and was applauded by W. Somerset Maugham and Pulitzer-Prize winner Thornton Wilder. It clearly deserved such accolades and showed Wescott at the top of his form.

*TheGrandmothers* was soon followed by the publication of *Goodbye, Wisconsin,* a collection of short stories. Among the many good stories in this collection, "Adolescence" is about a young boy who dresses up as a girl to attend a party where no one recognizes him and he is kissed by another boy. "A Guilty Woman" has a

**A terracotta bust of Glenway Wescott. Photo courtesy of the Wisconsin Historical Society. (WHi-2654)**

woman released from prison after serving her term for murdering a lover and returns to her hometown to live with another woman. "In A Thicket" tells of a young girl and her grandfather living in the woods at the edge of town. A black man has escaped from the nearby prison and the girl sees him prowling about the house.

The best story is "The Whistling Swan." A man and a woman — both young — exchange letters over a period of years until, when the time comes for them to meet again, he is worried: "Failing to love her now would be unfaithfulness not only to her, but to a work of his imagination." Then he shoots a swan by accident and is haunted by its scream.

In Paris, Wescott and Wheeler returned to the social round, a pattern that continued the rest of their lives. Between 1929 and 1933, Wescott published three books, all of which did not live up to the promise of *The Grandmothers.* These were *The Babels Bed, Fear and Trembling* (about his travels through pre-war Germany and the rise of German nationalism), and *A Calendar of Saints for Unbelievers* (one of Wescott's rare stabs at humor). Wescott's male characters, frustrated by love, have an annoying tendency to break out in tears in the presence of women.

While in Paris, he met Katharine Anne Porter and they began a lifelong friendship, though they often disagreed about Wescott's gay lifestyle. Wescott returned to America in 1934, where his literary creativity seemed to dry up. Aside from a few essays and poems in *The New Yorker, Transatlantic Review* and others, he published nothing of significance. Many works were begun and abandoned. Some that he wrote, he dared not publish. He moved from New York to a farm, which he called Stone-blossom, in western New Jersey and later was forced by the construction of a water reservoir to move to another farm, Haymeadows, where he stayed for the rest of his life.

Finally, in 1940, Wescott produced *The Pilgrim Hawk.* Along with *The Grandmothers,* it is Wescott's best work, set among an odd cast of characters wandering about a grand house in a Paris suburb. The falcon itself becomes a symbol for human relationships.

World War II arrived and Wescott, who had begun keeping a journal, was obviously worried about his friends and companions still living in France. He wrote short stories set in occupied France and in 1945 published *Apartment in Athens,* which in tone and style was a total departure from Wescott's earlier works. More realistic and psychologically acute, Wescott's portrayal of Kalter, the German officer, and the Helianos, the Greek family he moves in with, is riveting.

*Apartment in Athens* also was his last work of fiction. Wescott was 44. Never in American letters has a person's career been broken so sharply into two halves. After *Apartment in Athens,* Wescott's creativity dried up again, this time for good. Instead, he devoted the rest of his life to helping other writers and artists. For the next forty years, Wescott became a public figurehead, a champion and rallying point for worthy causes. Elected to the American Academy — Institute of Arts and Letters in 1947, he became its president in 1957 and held the post until 1961. That same year, Wescott, who had met nearly every literary figure of his time, finally met Robert Frost. Wescott noted at the time: "I stood as though all soul, upon one of the great divides of my life."

Wescott also became involved in UNESCO and the New York Museum of Modern Art where he later served on the board. In 1962, he published his last book, *Images of Truth,* which had essays on his friends and contemporaries: Porter, Maugham, Wilder, Collette, Isak Dinesen and Thomas Mann. More essays were later published in various magazines, but the influence that Wescott made upon American literature is contained in the half-dozen novels he wrote between 1924 and 1945. His Wisconsin books are *The Apple of the Eye, The Grandmothers, Goodbye, Wisconsin* and *The Babels Bed.*

Glenway Wescott died at age 86 at his New Jersey home on February 22, 1987.

### GLENWAY WESCOTT: SELECTED READING
- *Goodbye, Wisconsin,* Harper & Brothers,New York. 1928.
- *The Grandmothers,* Harper & Brothers New York. 1927.
- *Apartment in Athens,* Harper & Brothers, New York. 1945.
- *Images of Truth,* Harper & Brothers, New York. 1962.
- *The Apple of the Eye,* The Dial Press, Chicago. 1924.
- *Continual Lessons,* Farrar, Strauss, Giroux, New York. 1990.

# ROBERT E. GARD

It took a farm boy from Kansas to show the world the special place that Wisconsin holds in the literature and folklore of America. As important in its way as Steinbeck's California, or Faulkner's Yoknap-atawpha County or Stephen King's Maine villages of Castle Rock and Derry, so was Robert Gard's decades-long quest to preserve and present the history and folklore of Wisconsin through his "Wisconsin Idea."

Robert E. Gard was born near Iola, Kansas in 1910. He spent his early youth on a farm where he soon became aware of the limited life that sprawled before him. When Gard was born, his father was almost 50, thus the brunt of the hard work fell upon his young shoulders. In Gard's semi-autobiography, *Coming Home To Wisconsin,* he recounts the day when he was told to leave home and make his own way in the world. One night, his father wandered out into the corn field to puff on his pipe and look at the stars. When young Bob is sent after him to bring him home, he finds his father in the small cemetery nearby and is told that it's time for the boy to seek "the Stranger."

Gard spent a whole summer searching for the Stranger. He worked on farms and road construction gangs and saw what the Depression had done to the men and women of his time, robbing their spirit and leaving them helpless and hollow-eyed. Having spent his whole life on the farm, the callow youth was easily led astray by the pitfalls of life on the road. He was set upon and robbed. Penniless, he found work with a strong-willed widow farm woman and later witnessed the gangster killing of his boss on the construction crew.

Finally, while helping load sandbags in Lawrence, Kansas to keep the Kaw River from flooding the town, Gard met a university professor, Allen Grafton, who took him under his wing and helped him develop his burgeoning desire to write down his experiences searching for the Stranger.

A short time later, Gard left Kansas and enrolled at Cornell University in Ithaca, New York. There, under the guidance of David Stevens, he began to write plays that were performed by the Cornell University Drama Club. Some of these plays reflected young Gard's talent for comedy. *Mixing Up The Rent* had its origins in a James Fennimore Cooper story, "Satanstoe." *Rent* is a comedic farce about the Anti-Rent Wars in New York State during the early 1800s when the tenants revolted and refused to pay their landlords.

*Raisin' the Devil* adapts an old folktale to a modern setting. Ren Dow is a well-known preacher who tries to convert a horse thief and his daughter, who has been seeing a young man on the sly. The young man is there when Dow visits and hides in a flour barrel. Dow waits until the horse thief returns and the horse thief agrees to convert if Ren can "raise the devil," upon which Ren sticks his cane into the flour barrel and out pops the young man, covered in flour and, screeching in fright, flees the house. Another play, *Let's Get On With The Marryin',* portrays the perils of marrying folks in the backwoods.

While at Cornell, in a production of Chekov's *Uncle Vanya,* Robert Gard met Maryo Kimball, whom he married in 1939. They stayed together until her death in 1984. In 1942, at the outbreak of World War II, Gard and Maryo moved to Alberta, Canada, where Gard spent the next three years developing the basis of what would later become the "Wisconsin Idea." As the director of the Alberta Local Folklore and History Project, he collected folk tales of the region which were later published as *Johnny Chinook: Tall Tales and True from the Canadian West.*

In 1945, Gard arrived in Madison, Wisconsin. He had been encouraged to seek a teaching job at the University of Wisconsin by another mentor at Cornell, Alexander Drummond. Gard stayed at the University of Wisconsin for nearly 40 years, becoming a prolific writer and collector of Wisconsin folklore.

*Wisconsin is my Doorstep* was published in 1948. Subtitled "A Dramatist's Yarn Book of Wisconsin Lore," this is a book long overdue for reprinting. *Wisconsin is my Doorstep* shines with Gard's love for the Badger State. Inside are tall tales and true tales about Wisconsin and its people. There's a log-skidding contest among lumberjacks, a visit by a Wisconsin woman to Abraham Lincoln to plead for better hospital conditions during the Civil War and a much-hyped duel between Wisconsin and Iowa involving cheese. There's also a plethora of folk sayings about the weather, the origin of the infamous Rhinelander hodag beast, an account of a miracle that occurred during the great Peshtigo fire of 1871 and the tale of a shipwreck on September 8, 1860, in which 300 people were lost on Lake Michigan. *Wisconsin is my Doorstep* is a fast, enjoyable read told with abundant folksy charm.

By 1948, Gard had developed his Wisconsin Idea to the point where he founded (with the help of a remarkable woman named Fidelia von Antwerp) the Wisconsin Rural Writers, a forerunner of the Wisconsin Regional Writers Association, which still exists today as a vital outlet for aspiring Wisconsin writers. "The Wisconsin Idea" was a term coined by Charles McCarthy, a University of Wisconsin history professor, to describe the socio-political ferment that raged through Wisconsin in the early 1900s and later was exemplified by Senator Robert LaFollette.

Other organizations that Gard either founded or helped to found during his long tenure at the University of Wisconsin were: the Wisconsin Idea Theatre, the Council for Wisconsin Writers, the Rhinelander School of Arts, the Wisconsin Arts Council and many more, all developed with the idea of collecting and preserving Wisconsin's oral and dramatic heritage. The culmination of Gard's life work can be found at the Robert E. Gard Wisconsin Idea Foundation at Aldebaran Farm in Spring Green, Wisconsin.

In the 1950s Gard began writing a series of children's books at the behest of "Cap" Pearce of the publishing firm Duell, Sloan, and Pearce. Most of these books were set in his native state of Kansas and reflected Gard's love of

**Robert Gard. Photo courtesy of *Wisconsin State Journal/Capital Times* newsroom library.**

horses.

*The Error of Sexton Jones* was Gard's first work of fiction. This short novel, published in 1964, is a lighthearted look at a church sexton who hears the "voice" of the church speaking to him. The church tells Samuel Jones of its impending doom at the hands of a new young priest who has visions of building a new church, aided by a ruthless insurance man who does favors for the local construction firm.

Sexton Jones's wife, Clara, naturally thinks he's going to pot, a bit off in the head. Eventually, the furor arising from Jones's spirited defense of the old church, St. Alban's, comes to the attention of the bishop. Jones is hauled before the venerable bishop and pleads his case, but, though the bishop is sympathetic — and all through the book the church reveals the secrets of the other men and women who oppose keeping the old building — Jones loses and the church building is torn down. A hidden dowry also comes into play that acts as the catalyst to the church's eventual destruction.

Gard collaborated on a book titled *The Romance of Wisconsin Place Names,* which chronicled the history of the naming of each Wisconsin town and village as well as numerous landmarks such as Devil's Lake and Horicon Marsh. Horicon Marsh became a favorite spot for Gard and he published a splendid book about it called *Wild Goose Marsh* in 1972 .

I met Gard at Horicon Marsh one summer day in either 1989 or 1990. I encountered him while walking along the wooden pontoon bridge deep in the marsh waters where cattails loomed well over our heads and the honking of geese could be heard for miles. We talked for a bit and he gave me a short history of the marshland.

Another Gard compendium was *Down in the Valleys: Wisconsin Back Country Lore and Humor,* published in 1971. These stories are set mostly in the southwestern part of Wisconsin, the Kickapoo River Valley and Grant and Iowa counties. In another book, *The Trail of the Serpent,* Gard went north to collect stories of the Fox River Valley.

Late in life, Robert Gard never stopped writing. *Coming Home To Wisconsin* and *Innocence of Prairie* are mostly autobiographical works. In the former book, Gard reflects that "retrospection can go anywhere your mind has ever been." In *Coming Home,* Gard alternates chapters of autobiography with accounts of Wisconsin history: the demise of the passenger pigeon, the legend of Chief Black Hawk, Robert La Follette. A most poignant chapter deals with the importance of elm trees in American life — most now gone due to Dutch Elm Disease.

Gard's final book was his most surprising. *Beyond the Thin Line* is a very personal and stark look at Alzheimer's disease. A longtime friend of Gard's, Harry MacDare, got Alzheimer's and Gard spent long hours and many days with Harry, chronicling the steady and insidious advance of the disease as Harry lost his memory piece by piece. There are many tender moments, especially when one fully realizes that there are so many memories for Harry, who was a prisoner-of-war in World War II and also a postal worker for 35 years, that are slowly slipping away.

Shortly after *Beyond the Thin Line* was published in 1992, Gard passed away at the age of 81.

### ROBERT E. GARD: SELECTED READING
- *Wisconsin is My Doorstep: A Dramatist's Yarn Book of Wisconsin Lore,* Longmans, Green & Co. New York. 1948.
- *The Error of Sexton Jones,* Duell, Sloan, and Pearce, New York, 1964.
- *The Romance of Wisconsin Place Names,* Wisconsin House, 1969. (reprinted in 1988 by Heartland Press of Minocqua, Wisconsin)
- *Down in the Valleys: Wisconsin Back Country Lore and Humor,* Wisconsin House, 1971.
- *Wild Goose Marsh: Horicon Stopover,* Wisconsin House, 1972.
- *A Woman of No Importance,* Wisconsin House, 1974.
- *Coming Home to Wisconsin,* Stanton & Lee, 1982.
- *Beyond the Thin Line,* Prairie Oak Press, 1992.

# T.V. OLSEN

The best-selling westerns of today are not the traditional westerns written by the old guard: Max Brand, Zane Grey or even Louis L'Amour. Today's westerns eschew the staples of the old-style western melodramas: the white-hat hero, the black-garbed villain, the damsel in distress. Instead they are more concerned with historical figures portrayed with all their warts and weaknesses.

Wisconsin's most famous writer of westerns was T.V. Olsen. He lived nearly all of his life in the North Woods, but Olsen was among the first western writers who began to drift away from the traditional western story and tackle themes prevalent in western fiction today.

Theodore Victor Olsen was born in Rhinelander in 1932, a fourth-generation member of his family in the Rhinelander area. Olsen attended classes in the Rhinelander public school system and, in his own words, his childhood was unremarkable except for his preoccupation with reading novels by Zane Grey and Edgar Rice Burroughs.

While in high school, Olsen had ambitions of becoming a professional cartoonist in the style of Walt Kelly, creator of the "Pogo" comic strip. He took a night class in creative writing, which led him to change his goal to that of becoming a writer.

Olsen graduated from high school in 1950 and enrolled at Central State College in Stevens Point where in his junior year he began work on a novel. In 1954, he sent the manuscript to the August Lenniger Literary Agency. Six months later, he received a letter and critique from John Burr, formerly an editor of *Western Story*, one of the popular pulp magazines at the time.

Three months after Olsen had graduated from college with a bachelor's degree, the novel sold to Ace Books, where it appeared in 1956 as *Haven of the Hunted*. His first published short story was bought and adapted for the television series "Dick Powell's Zane Grey Theatre" in 1957.

About this time, T.V. Olsen wrote down his views of western fiction in a magazine article. He wrote that modern western fiction required better plot development while still adhering to the traditional elements of the Western.

The next four years proved hard ones for Olsen. With the virtual disappearance of the pulp markets his only successes were stories that appeared in "Ranch Romances" and a second Western novel, *The Man From Nowhere,* which appeared in 1959.

Olsen became a regular author for Gold Medal Books, beginning with the sale of *McGivern* in 1960. He followed that with three more novels in quick succession and his career held to a fairly regular path from that time. He was now considered a known Western author.

T.V. Olsen took his first trip out West in 1961. He was to return frequently thereafter. Unusual in this regard, most of Olsen's Western stories took place in lonely, isolated areas far from a town. The land itself plays a prominent role in Olsen's work, whereas stories set in a town reflect more on the characters who live there.

One story that Olsen wrote, "Five Minutes," is set in the North Woods of Wisconsin. It concerns a wrongly convicted man who breaks prison and is on his way to seek revenge against the corrupt politician who framed him. In the woods, he meets a young girl who becomes convinced that the man is innocent. When the story didn't sell, Olsen changed the setting to the 1880s West and the title to "Journey of No Return" and it promptly sold as his second published western story.

In 1970, Olsen married Jacqueline Brooks Michalek, but their marriage soon ended in divorce. At the time, Olsen was spending long hours researching and writing his first major historical novel, *There Was A Season,* which portrays young Jefferson Davis during the years 1832-1833 when he was an Army lieutenant on the Wisconsin frontier and Davis's bittersweet love affair with Sarah Knox Taylor, daughter of Zachary Taylor, later hero of the Mexican War and president of the United States.

While researching this period, Olsen read Beverly

Butler's *Feather in the Wind,* published in 1965 and set in Wisconsin in 1832. Their correspondence soon bloomed into romance.

Blind since the age of 14 due to glaucoma, Beverly had gone on to earn a master's degree from Marquette University and had already established herself as an author of young adult fiction. They were married in 1976.

The books and stories continued. Olsen had quickly mastered the craft of writing the western and often wrote under a pen name as well. He continued to experiment with traditional Western themes in his stories.

Olsen's supernatural western, "Jacob's Journal," was written at the behest of Joe Lansdale, a popular horror writer who also wrote about the Old West, for a publishing project which, sadly, never came about. The story later appeared in Louis L'Amour's *Western Magazine.*

Off-beat, even for Olsen, "Jacob's Journal" concerns an unscrupulous trader who sells unfit cattle to the local Indian reservation.

One of Olsen's early novels, *Break the Young Land,* is a taut, tight story about Norwegian and Swedish immigrants moving to the Kansas prairie from Koshkonong, Wisconsin. Borg Vikstrom is a stalwart Norske who must keep the settlers and the newly arrived Texas cowboys from violence. His task is complicated by Eben Haggard, a New England land speculator who is using both factions for his own purposes.

In another novel, *Track the Man Down,* Olsen's main character is an African American who is being hunted by a white posse. Olsen does a masterful job of portraying the African American viewpoint of how life for blacks really was in the Old West.

A later novel, *Deadly Pursuit,* tells the story of Silas Pine, a mountain man returning to see his wife and son whom he had abandoned many years before. While entering town, Silas foils a bank robbery and saves his son's life. However, when the posse catches up with the surviving robbers, Noah Pine is killed. Silas vows revenge, but there is more here than meets the eye. The bank president has his own reasons for wanting the last robber dead as does the new acting marshal, Isom Rastrow. Silas is drawn to the wife and child of the last surviving robber and he is forced to join with the wife, Shawn, in pursuing her husband. The book has several nicely portrayed black and Indian characters.

Two of T.V. Olsen's western novels were made into films. *The Stalking Moon* starred Gregory Peck as an Army scout on his last patrol who discovers a white woman and her children amidst the ruins of an Indian camp after an attack. The woman's Apache husband was a noted warrior, Salvaje (The Ghost), who was now looking for revenge against the Army and wants to recover his two children, the older of which admires Salvaje and seeks to return to his natural father.

*Arrow in the Sun* was filmed as "Soldier Blue" and starred Candace Bergen as a saucy New York woman who came west to be an Army wife. She had recently escaped from spending two years as a captive of the Cheyenne. Honus Gant is a raw recruit and with Cresta Lee are the only survivors of the massacre of an Army pay wagon.

Thematically, *Arrow in the Sun* is similar to *The Stalking Moon*. Cresta's Cheyenne husband, Spotted Wolf, also comes seeking her, and both novels end with a climactic duel between the white man and the Indian.

T.V. Olsen also wrote historical adventure novels in a different setting. One of these is *Treasures of the Sun*. It involves a 1922 expedition to discover a lost city of the Incas and the supposed remnants of a surviving Inca people and their hoarded gold. This is very much in the style of the H.. Rider Haggard adventure novels. A second novel, *The Lost Colony*, is set in the Pacific Northwest.

Along with his Westerns and historical adventures, T.V. Olsen did not neglect his Wisconsin roots. He began a series of books under the title *The Rhinelander Country* which chronicled the history of the Rhinelander area from its geological beginnings to its role today as a vacation spot.

*Volume One: Roots of the North* takes the history up to the point immediately after the Civil War, while *Volume Two:*

*Birth of a City* revels in the boom days of the North Woods logging industry from 1870 to 1900 and shortly thereafter.

T.V. Olsen died on July 13, 1993. Since his death, he has acquired a notable following among western readers and many of his earlier books have been reprinted and some, written under his pen-name, have been published for the first time. For a North Woods boy, T.V. Olsen captured the vista of the Old West as well as anybody.

### T.V. OLSEN: SELECTED READING
- *Break the Young Land,* 1964 (1990, Chivers Press, Bath, England).
- *The Stalking Moon,* 1965. Doubleday & Co., New York.
- *Arrow in the Sun,* 1969. Doubleday & Co., New York.
- *There Was a Sea-Son,* 1971 (1994, Leisure Books, New York).
- *Deadly Pursuit,* 1995. Five Star Western, Unity, Maine.
- *Lone Hand: Frontier Stories,* 1997. Five Star Western, Unity, Maine.
- *Treasures of the Sun,* 1998. Five Star Western, Unity, Maine.
- *Roots of the North,* 1979, Pineview Publishing, Rhinelander, Wisconsin.
- *Birth of a City,* 1983, Pineview Publishing, Rhinelander, Wisconsin.

# THORNTON WILDER

When Thornton Wilder was 13, he received a letter from his father: "Thornton: you must write your best when you take pen in hand. For a thirteen-year-old your handwriting is faulty. Even as you grow older you may remain a little boy in heart."

Some would say that Thornton Wilder did remain a little boy at heart, but he also wrote some very adult novels and, for a time, he was one of the greatest writers of his generation. He was the only writer to win a Pulitzer Prize for both fiction and drama, a three-time Pulitzer Prize winner and had a reputation as an American writer with a European style.

Thornton Wilder's parents, Amos and Isabella Nevin Wilder, moved to Wisconsin from New York in 1894. Amos Wilder bought a quarter interest in the *Wisconsin State Journal* newspaper. He wrote editorials for the paper and was hard-edged in his judgements. Thornton Wilder was born in Madison on April 17, 1897. A frail child at birth, he quickly overcame this handicap and by the time he was three Wilder was the usual active boy. The family lived on Langdon Street and owned a summer cottage near the shores of Lake Mendota.

The Wilders lived in Madison until 1906 when Amos Wilder accepted a post as an attache to the U.S. Government in Hong Kong. After six months, Isabella took the four children, including Thornton, and sailed on *The Siberia* back to San Francisco. She settled in Berkeley where Wilder went to school and grew into a lean, black-haired, blue-eyed 12-year-old who was fluent in French, Italian, and German.

In 1910, Isabella returned to China with Thornton and his two sisters. They settled in Chefoo, but this sojourn lasted less than a year before Isabella insisted on visiting Italy. Thornton stayed behind in China and became the official letter-writer to the widely dispersed family. Moving yet again, Thornton returned to Berkeley and attended high school. There he wrote his first play "The Advertisement League" for a vaudeville show. Another play, "Captain Cecilia" found Wilder stretching out his talent into longer dramas.

After high school, Wilder went to Oberlin College in Ohio. There he took readily to the free and easy college life. He wrote a series of three-minute plays that showed an early bent for the religious and the fantastic: *Brother Fire, Prosperina and the Devil, Nascuntur Poetae, Childe Roland to the Dark Tower Came* and *And The Sea Shall Give Up Its Dead.*

By this time Amos and Isabella Wilder were together again in New Haven, Connecticut. After two years at Oberlin, Thornton transferred to Yale. The stricter life of a *Yalie* almost led to Wilder's downfall. He neglected his studies in favor of attending plays. One of his friends there was Stephen Vincent Benet.

After a short stint in the Coast Guard, which he spent mostly typing and drilling, Wilder returned to Yale in the fall of 1918. He wrote reviews for the *Boston Transcript* for grocery money. Upon graduating from Yale, Wilder found himself basically unfit for any type of career. Amos Wilder gave him $900 and sent him off to Italy to assist a friend in an archaeological dig. Wilder fell in love with Italy. Staying at the American Academy in Rome, he spent days roaming the countryside, enraptured by the ancient ruins and the aura of history permeating the Italian landscape. He briefly became a tour guide but then his stay in Rome ended after just eight months. Wilder then moved on to Paris. But Wilder's stay in Paris was also short. His inability to get a job was affecting his mental outlook.

Thornton bounced to Lawrenceville, New Jersey, to teach French at a finishing school for young boys on their way to Princeton. Wilder was now 24 years old. He began work on a novel that he originally titled *Memoirs of A Roman Student* but later, when the manuscript was accepted by Albert and Charles Boni, publishers out of New York,

**Thornton Wilder. Photo courtesy of Wisconsin Historical Society. (WHi-2655)**

the title was changed to *The Cabala.*

*The Cabala* begins with a descriptive passage of the Italian landscape and some of the people he comes across. The narrator, Samuele, seeks knowledge of a mysterious Italian cabala or secret society. He befriends a young prince named Marcantonio, but the prince commits suicide after a fight with his sister, the Duchess Julia. Wilder has a fine sense of nature writing that evokes the graceful prose of Walter Pater.

We move on to Princess Alix D'Esposi, a cultured and dazzling young woman doomed to a series of unhappy love affairs. Samuele's companion in Rome is an American named James Blair, who has buried himself in Rome's history. Alix and Blair fall in love, but the union is fraught with disaster. Blair flees to England while Alix, after a chance encounter with Samuele at a confessional, resumes her old ways.

Another member of the cabala is Astree-Luce de Morfontaine, a religious woman who is unsteady in her faith because she has never suffered or been tested. She and Cardinal Vaini have long admired each other, but when the cardinal puts Astree-Luce's faith on trial, she fails miserably and shoots at him. The action is forgiven, but the cardinal dies at sea on his way to China.

Wilder began a correspondence with a married woman, Amy Weil Wertheimer, and their platonic relationship lasted for most of his life. When *The Cabala* was published in 1926, it met with critical acclaim and modest sales. Wilder was already hard at work on his second novel, *The Bridge of San Luis Rey*. He spent all of July writing from nine in the morning until three in the afternoon, then went to Europe for the fall where he settled in Paris and continued work. In January 1927, he returned to New Haven where his vagabond life continued.

In biographies, it is always fun to read about the author's first breakthrough novel. The reader can get caught up in the excitement just as if it had happened only yesterday. Thornton Wilder's *The Bridge of San Luis Rey* became overnight a best-seller and won the Pulitzer Prize in 1928.

The novel begins with the bridge, which spans a gorge outside of Lima, Peru. It suddenly snaps and collapses, hurtling five people to their deaths. The accident is witnessed by the narrator, Brother Juniper, who resolves to capture the human essence of every one of the five victims. The first is the Dona Maria, *marquesa de montemayor* and her surrogate daughter, Pepita. Pepita had been plucked from an orphanage, but in Dona Maria's care, life was still not easy.

Esteban and his brother Manuel were twins living in Lima. They had also been in the convent with Madre Maria de Pilar until they were teenagers, and then they went about the city as laborers and dockworkers. Manuel had a talent for writing and he wrote letters for a famous actress La

Perichole. At last, Manuel, torn by his love for La Perichole, refuses to write any more letters. A day later, he cuts his leg and gangrene sets in. Manuel dies and Esteban is shattered. He finally agrees to go on a sea voyage but is caught crossing the bridge at the moment of collapse.

Uncle Pio possessed the six attributes of the adventurer — a memory for names and faces, with the aptitude for altering his own; the gift of tongues; inexhaustible invention; secrecy; the ability to fall into conversation with strangers; and that freedom of conscience that springs from a contempt for the dozing rich he preyed upon.

Pio was the agent and guardian of La Perichole, the actress. As La Perichole ages and gives up the theater, Pio hangs around trying to lure her back. Pio is given La Perichole's young son, Jaime, to train, but both of them meet their fate on the bridge.

For all his pains in writing this account, Brother Juniper is seized by the Spanish and burned to death, thus ending the book.

Meanwhile, Boni had published Wilder's collection of short playlets, *The Angel That Troubled The Waters,* which was also selling well. His younger sister Isabel was now a constant companion and personal secretary. Drawn to Chicago by the offer of a teaching position, Wilder finally forced himself into a set schedule, and between 1930 and 1936 cemented his standing as one of America's foremost authors and playwrights. Among his friends during his Chicago period was the actress Ruth Gordon. He also made friends with Gertrude Stein, then living in Paris, and often corresponded with her. Unfortunately, after a lifetime of abstinence, Wilder began drinking; he "enjoyed the bustle after five o'clock" and the older he got the more he drank.

Gilbert Harrison, in *The Enthusiast: A Life of Thornton Wilder* offers up this summary of Wilder's writings to this point:

"[*The Woman of Andros*] is a more compressed novel than *The Bridge,* but the question it raises is common to all of Thornton's work: when a situation is more than a human soul can be expected to bear, what then? *The Cabala* was a series of three such extremities, *The Bridge* implied that at the heart of love there lies an intuition that offers sufficient strength for crises. *The Woman of Andros* asks whether paganism has any answer for the inquiring sufferer and, by anticipation, whether the maxims that entered the world with the message of Christianity are an adequate guide." (p. 142)

*The Woman of Andros* is a story set in ancient Greece. Simo and Chremes are parents of two young lovers. The young man, Pamphilus, is 25 and apparently reluctant to marry. One night Simo is approached by a mysterious woman who has been the target of island gossip. Her name is Chrysis and she wishes to send money via Simo to an old sea captain friend of hers. As in the later play, *Our Town,* Wilder sets up the story of a person offered the chance to relive one day of their life all over again — "the most un-eventful day."

Chrysis has a daughter named Glycerium who one day meets with Pamphilus. They fall in love but are constrained by Greek customs. Chrysis sickens and dies and Glycerium is sold into slavery. At the last moment she is rescued by Simo and Pamphilus, but she dies in childbirth. Despite this gloomy ending, *The Woman of Andros* is a beautifully written story.

In between novels, Wilder was still writing plays. *The Long Christmas Dinner* is an interesting little play spanning ninety years in the life of one particular family. *The Queens of France* is an amusing little bagatelle. In *Pullman Car Hiawatha* Wilder has the stage manager bring out the Components of Time: "The minutes are gossips; the hours are philosophers; the years are theologians. The hours are philosophers with the exception of Twelve O'Clock who is also a theologian." (p. 62)

Wilder went to Hollywood to write several screen treatments for such stars as Katharine Hepburn, Fredric March, Lillian Gish, Marlene Dietrich and others. But movies were mere sidelines for Wilder. After the publication of *Heaven's My Destination,* Wilder resigned from teaching at the University of Chicago and went to Switzerland to concentrate on finishing his first full-length play, *Our Town*.

*Heaven's My Destination* is Thornton Wilder's modern take on Bunyan's *Pilgrim's Progress*. Youthful, inexperienced George Brush is out on the road selling school books. He is a markedly religious man with certain fixed ideas that don't bode well with his inability to blend in with a crowd. His attempt to withdraw his money from a bank leads him to wind up in jail. George attends a summer camp where he meets with a serious-minded girl, or so he thinks. But when she reveals that she is a proponent of evolution, contrary to George's fundamentalist beliefs, he is dismayed. The story is set at the height of the Depression, so George has to find many means of travel — except on Sunday, that is. While at the camp, he befriends a suicidal businessman named Dick Roberts and appoints himself the fellow's guardian. In true serio-comic style, Wilder has George follow Roberts all night long despite Roberts' protestations.

Like Bunyan's work, George Brush wanders the world, prey to all temptations. Because of his naivete, he unwittingly gets drunk and visits a bordello and winds up taking all the women to a movie. When apprised of their real nature, George turns self-righteous and winds up in the hospital where everyone believe he is crazy. After getting arrested again, this time for participating in a robbery, George explains his emulation of Gandhi and the concept of ahimsa . Strangely, this leads to George himself losing his faith. He seeks out an old flame, a waitress named Roberta, and persuades her to marry him. George has also accepted the care of a young girl, Elizabeth. The marriage is an abysmal failure. George stubbornly refuses to budge from his ideals, which now seem the only source of stability left to him. The novel ends unsatisfyingly with George now back at the beginning, minus wife and daughter.

In a letter to Gertrude Stein, Wilder notes: "I am writing the most beautiful little play you can imagine. Every morning brings an hour's increment to it and that's all. But I've finished two acts already. It's a little play with all the big subjects in it; and it's a big play with all the little things of life lovingly impressed into it." ( *The Enthusiast*, p. 177)

*Our Town* is, along with *The Matchmaker*, Thornton Wilder's best- known play. Never does a year pass when *Our Town* isn't performed somewhere in America. On the surface, one wonders what it is about the play that resonates so strongly in our consciousness. The first act presents scenes of daily life as the people of Grover's Corners, New Hampshire, meet each other on the street at sunrise. Young George Gibbs is a baseball player who wants to farm his uncle's land; there's also the newspaper editor, the police officer, a young girl who dreams of a better life, and other characters. The narrative that ties all these people together is provided by the stage manager.

While the first act was set in 1901, Act Two takes place three years later. Act Three begins at the Grover's Corners cemetery nine years after that.

*Our Town* had a rough beginning. It flopped when first performed in Boston, but succeeded when it moved to New York. Wilder and producer Jed Harris fought over money and rights. In partial response, Wilder's next play was a farcical satire on business titled *The Merchant of Yonkers*. Rewritten much later and with the title changed to *The Matchmaker*, the play would be another great success and in 1964 would become the movie *Hello, Dolly!*

*The Skin Of Our Teeth* is Wilder's most baroque and offbeat play. Wilder plays around with biblical figures and events, predating Monty Python by 50 years. The audience has to be patient with all these goings on until Act Two, when the story begins to take shape. Mr. Antrobus, the president of the world, in the moments before a big broadcast announcing the imminent approach of a major storm, decides to leave his wife for a younger woman. The scene takes place in Atlantic City.

Act Three is set just after a terrible war. People have emerged from their underground hideaways. What follows is a parable of good and evil set amidst a backdrop of philosophy and the stars at night.

The outbreak of World War II changed Thornton Wilder. His writing fell off as he devoted more and more time to helping others in war relief efforts and goodwill missions.

He traveled to South America, visiting for the first time the Peru he chronicled in *The Bridge of San Luis Rey*. While *The Skin Of Our Teeth* was in production, Wilder was drafted into the Army. He became an intelligence officer and would spend most of his time in North Africa and Italy. One of Wilder's more unusual duties was to oversee the production of *Our Town* in Belgrade, Yugoslavia. When Germany surrendered on May 7, 1945, Thornton Wilder was 48.

In *The Ides of March*, Wilder returns to the form of an experimental novel.

Wilder in his fifties led a gypsy life. He traveled back and forth to Europe, visiting friends, working on translations of plays (including the works of Jean-Paul Sartre), being feted and even taking to the stage himself, playing Mr. Antrobus in *The Skin Of Our Teeth*. In 1950, Wilder accepted a visiting professorship at Harvard University. From this would come his posthumously published book *American Characteristics and Other Essays*. Wilder's last play, *The Alcestiad*, was a complete failure and led him to withdraw from public life. He became cranky about his fame, telling friends that he despised a television program to be shown about his life and that people were foolish to claim he was "a thinker with a message for our times."

During the 1960s, Wilder wrote a few minor plays. The success of *Hello, Dolly!* in 1964 caught him by surprise and led to his resumption of a novel, *The Eighth Day*.

The story begins in Coaltown, Illinois, where John Ashley stands trial for the murder of his friend and business partner Breckenridge Lansing. The year is 1902. Ashley is sentenced to death, but on the train to Joliet prison, he is rescued by a mysterious group of men, given a horse, and flees to South America. Left behind is a wife, a son and three daughters.

When it was published in 1967, *The Eighth Day* met with mostly harsh reviews. Wilder had become out-of-date and his type of novels were no longer either being written.

By 1970, Thornton Wilder's health was failing. His eyes were weak and a lifetime of cigarette smoking left him short of breath. He managed to write one more novel, an excellent picaresque story called *Theophilus North,* which was published in 1973.

On December 6, 1975, Wilder spent the morning at the Harvard Club, then went home. In the afternoon he took a nap, and when his sister Isabel went to waken him for dinner, she found him dead. He was 78.

### THORNTON WILDER: SELECTED READING

- *The Long Christmas Dinner and Other Plays in One Act,* 1932, Coward- McCann, New York. 122 pp.
- *Heaven's My Destination,* 1934, Harper & Brothers, New York. 304 pp.
- *Thornton Wilder Trio: The Bridge of San Luis Rey, The Cabala, The Woman of Andros,* 1956, Criterion Books, New York. 309 pp.
- *The Eighth Day,* 1967, Harper & Row, New York. 435 pp.
- *Theophilus North,* 1973, Harper & Row, New York. 374 pp.
- *Three Plays: Our Town, The Skin of Our Teeth, The Matchmaker,* 1998, Perennial Classics/Harper Row. 431 pp.
- *The Enthusiast: A Life of Thornton Wilder,* by Gilbert A. Harrison. 1983, Ticknor & Fields, New York. 403 pp.

# WARREN BECK

In my opinion, the finest short story writer Wisconsin has yet produced was Warren Beck. Beck wrote of people in love, but his people did not remain static, tied to one place — they moved on. Some of his short stories are masterpieces, and it is sad to think that he has been forgotten over the years.

Warren Beck was born in Richmond, Indiana, in 1896. Not much is known of his early life beyond the fact that he began writing at a young age. He attended Earlham College in Richmond and then went to Columbia University in New York. In 1926, he moved to Wisconsin, where he began teaching on the English faculty at Lawrence College in Appleton. By 1939, his short stories were beginning to get some recognition. "The Blue Sash" was reprinted in Edward J. O'Brien's *Best Short Stories of 1939*. Many writers had their first taste of fame by appearing in these anthologies in which the stories were rated on a five-star system. By 1941, Beck had written enough stories for a collection, *The Blue Sash and Other Stories,* published by Antioch Press of Yellow Springs, Ohio.

Early on in this collection Warren Beck exhibits a flair for the snappy candid dialogue prevalent in 1920s and 1930s fiction. "The Blue Sash" tells about two fellows planning to go out to Los Angeles to seek their fortune. One is almost engaged to a girl but has his doubts. His friend stokes his ambition with lines like: "Once in Los Angeles, we could line up something that would feed us while we investigate the customs and cuties of Aimee McPherson's diocese." (p. 14). But just as Bob was packing to leave he glances out the window to see a woman walking across the street in a pink dress with a blue sash. He changes his mind and decides to settle down after all.

In "The Shadow of A Green Olive Tree," a patient uncle teachers a lesson about mortality and how time passes. Two young lovers try each other out on an excursion through the city in "No Nightingale." Each reveals that the other, while not exactly ideal, is acceptable.

"Jake Boyd" is a wonderful story about a man who returns to his hometown after a long absence and looks up an old friend, once a vaudeville manager, now the owner of a movie theater in the same building. Personally, the story awakened a lot of memories for me. "Jake Boyd" is a story of a man caught up in the past, trapped by memories that won't fade.

"Unity, Coherence, and..." tells of a rigorous English teacher who refuses the temptation to bend his standards. "Not Without Dust and Heat" involves a love affair between a scholarly type who is flirting with socialism and a businessman's wife. He discovers that he enjoys "the thrill of the chase" after all. Another story, "Needle's Eye," is a dramatic psychological account of an apparent class war between a hard German and his more easy-going fellow Americans. Written after Hitler's rise to power, it's a revealing portrait of the way people view themselves as superior to others. The story's violent ending presages the Holocaust.

"Where The Apple Reddens" is an excellent, witty story about an advertising salesman and his well-along pregnant wife on a car journey to visit her mother. All during the drive Beck interweaves snippets from classical literature — Eliot, Shakespeare, Whitman — which play through the man's mind in rapid-fire free associative fashion. At the end of the journey, the scene turns more romantic and formal — but beautiful.

On a different track is "Encounter On A Parnassian Slope." Once again the main character, Stanley Roberts, is an advertising copywriter. He has just received a rejection of his novel from a publishing firm but is urged to go see the famous novelist Hugh Kent. Though cordial at first, Kent soon reveals a morbidly sensual side that revolts Roberts. As Roberts walks away, he uses his advertising talent, not his novelist's eye, to begin another subject.

A noteworthy aspect of Warren Beck's short stories is that each one is different and contains different surprises.

"Generations" begins with a spat between an older brother and younger sister over who is to have the family car on a Saturday night date. The young lad, having won his argument, visits his grandfather's room and browses through the old books. This brings about reflective ruminations on his grandfather's life and leads to a wholly satisfying and adult conclusion.

Beck also has a deep feeling for humanity as seen in the story "The Little Jap." Told by an omniscient third person, the figure of Sahago, in most other hands, could turn into stereotypically inscrutable Asian, but Beck deftly portrays the nuances involved in this clash between traditional Japanese customs and a rowdy, obnoxious American college student. Written during Christmas week in 1938, "The Little Jap" ends with an eerie premonition — perhaps even a cautionary note — of the reasons behind the bombing of Pearl Harbor three years later.

*The Blue Sash and Other Stories* closes with another beautiful and moving tale about a young man bringing a girlfriend back to his hometown. They visit the cemetery where his parents are buried and the house where he grew up. Although she is not religious, she wants to experience a Catholic Mass. This Mass is in Latin, and we see everything through her eyes. She notices how much the ancient ceremony has taken hold of his emotions and gets up to leave, but he follows after her.

In 1944 came Beck's first attempt at a novel. *Final Score*, the story of a dying athlete, was modestly received, but lacked the sharp focus that Warren Beck brings to his short stories. He returned in 1947 with another collection, *The First Fish and Other Stories*. Many writers have explored the thrill of catching their first fish. Warren Beck gives this simple tale a tinge of mysticism, even amidst the clinical prose describing the ritual killing and cleaning of the catch. It is a boy's journey into new knowledge and an instant that might shape his future life.

A personal war against injustice flavors the story "Out of Line." A man is waiting in a long line at the post office, waiting to send his son, fighting in the war, a box of hard candy. A well-to-do woman dressed in fox furs, obviously impatient and accustomed to having her way, tries to cut in line ahead of several people. The man protests, but later reflects on whether his actions did any real good.

Another favorite Beck story is "Fire and Branch," a seemingly innocuous tale of a young boy being jilted by a flighty girl while ice skating. Yet the experience has taught him something, and he reaches out to others now instead of retreating to his own enclosed world. "Between Friends" reveals that once Death has entered the picture, nothing can ever be the same.

"Boundary Line," published in 1942 in the early days of World War II, depicts the tensions between an American couple and the German family, the Schwartz's, who live next door with a hedge separating their yards. Suspicions mount as the German family turns more reclusive, and the resolution to the story is not what one might expect.

Another war-time story is "Beyond The Brow Of The Hill." On a routine shopping trip, a man meets a middle-aged woman burdened by her bags. He offers her his seat on the bus, and for the rest of the journey she tells of the upcoming marriage of her daughter to a recently returned soldier.

An odd little piece is "Sensible," about a prim woman, set in her ways, who suddenly begins to live impulsively. She buys a pair of Hansel and Gretel wooden figures for her garden, and she begins to treat them as if they were real children — until, that is, she comes to her senses.

"Poison in Jest" is a light piece about an office prank a conniving employer pulls on his loyal secretary. It backfires in a big way. Another excellent Beck story is "The Four-Faced God," which follows a chance encounter at a train station between a man and a woman who were formerly part of a group that dated and spent time together years before. Each has gone on to get married and have children, but Alan is still held by "what might have been."

"Six In A Booth" is a more political story with discussions of labor and unions; six people arguing their differing viewpoints until it is apparent that they will never get together again. "Today, The Road" finds a man visiting a long-time friend whose wife is gravely ill. They discuss her life as an artist until the moment comes when she dies. The friend then kills himself by taking poison from the doctor's medical bag. "On The Way" ends this collection with a beautiful story of a sailor meeting a woman on a train journey and they share confidences, finding much in common, but she already has a fine fellow, so he must continue the search. The last paragraph is a splendid statement of love and friendship.

In the same year (1947), Beck published another novel, *Pause Under The Sky*. Like his first novel, it was warmly received by the critics. In 1951, Beck again had two books released at the same time: a third novel called *Into Thin Air* and a short story collection, *The Far Whistle and Other Stories*.

"The Far Whistle" begins with a father taking his son to the beach to swim. There is also an old-fashioned train that circles the area, and the father notices the old man who is the engineer of the train and who dresses in the traditional garb. Intrigued, he asks the owner of the train ride about the old man and is given the background: how the fellow had farmed all his life but always wanted to be a railroad man. This was the next best thing. A nice little story.

On a darker note is "No Continuing City," which involves a favorite Beck theme: two old friends getting together after a long separation. This time, however, the forces of time and opinion have left them far apart and there is no common ground anymore. Another dark tale is "Edge of Doom," which features a sinister best- selling novelist and the young fragile artist he ruthlessly destroys. Yet fate has a hand in the author's future as well, and the story leaves more questions than answers.

"Verdict of Innocence" is a penetrating portrait of the human propensity to be a slave to Time and how it often washes out the joy in life. When Grampa sees Ruby scolding her young son Paul, he realizes that she is trapped by her actions, judged by the hectic pace of modern times. "Men Working" conjures up images of Jack Lemmon and

Walter Matthau playing the roles of slick advertising writers who must create interest in a failing movie. They find a street wino and sober him up, presenting his new condition as a result of seeing the movie. It's all slapstick comedy and a refreshing change from the previous stories.

Not many writers describe meeting a woman as Beck does in "The Clean Platter." The story itself involves two men who meet at a bar and share a tray of pretzels. For a moment the story seems to be straying into the macabre in the manner of Lord Dunsany's "Two Bottles of Relish," but it ends on a different note with Beck's by-now-familiar blend of wry humor.

"All Brothers Are Men" poses an interesting question of guilt and conscience amongst the members of a college fraternity after an incident causes official censure. A case study of the proper recourse involving a collective unanimity among disparate entities.

In a more cosmic vein is "Shadow of Turning." A man takes his young son to a planetarium show. First they see the planets revolve around the sun, then it's upstairs to see the stars in the darkened room. On the way back, they again pass the room where the planets are still revolving because someone had forgotten to shut them down. His son's casual comment brings back a memory.

"Felix" is a strange account of a man apparently fortifying himself with a secluded retreat in case the world ends. After all this hullabaloo. "Ask Me No More" poses a literary mystery. A chemistry student doing an English assignment finds himself baffled by the life of a notorious poet, now deceased. "The Child Is Father" takes a new angle on how a mother should raise her son. It is similar to the earlier story "Verdict of Innocence."

"Years Brought To An End" chronicles a visit by a youngish man to his elderly aunt. He meets his former school superintendent who has taken to chasing young girls. When Mr. Cooper is killed, along with a young girl, in an auto accident, the town is seen as wishing to publicly preserve his good standing while gossiping over the scandal.

"Detour In The Dark" is a novella about a man and his young son on their way home when they are forced to detour to a small town named Adam's Corners.

Warren Beck continued to teach at Lawrence University until his retirement in 1961. He also spent time as a visiting professor in England, Colorado, and Minnesota. In 1963 he published a fourth collection of short stories, *The Rest Is Silence and Other Stories*. Beck was also known as a scholar and published works on William Faulkner ( *Man In Motion: Faulkner's Trilogy*, 1961), James Joyce (Joyce's *Dubliners: Substance, Vision & Art* ), and Mark Twain.

After a long life, Warren Beck died in 1985. His short stories deserve to be reprinted.

**WARREN BECK: SELECTED READING**

• *The Blue Sash and Other Stories,* 1941, Antioch Press, Yellow Springs, Ohio. 198 pp.

• *The First Fish and Other Stories,* 1947, Antioch Press, Yellow Springs, Ohio. 212 pp.

• *The Far Whistle and Other Stories,* 1951, Antioch Press, Yellow Springs, Ohio. 224 pp.

# LORINE NIEDECKER

Lorine Niedecker was born on May 12, 1903 in Fort Atkinson, Wisconsin. Her father Henry was a hunter and fisherman who rented out cabins to other hunters and her mother Theresa, known as Daisy, suffered from hearing problems and went completely deaf in the last years of her life. Lorine spent most of her childhood outdoors, roaming Black Hawk island and Lake Koshkonong environs, observing "redwinged blackbirds, willows, maples, boats, fishing (the smell of tarred nets), twittering and squawking noises from the marsh." She attended Fort Atkinson High School and Beloit College in 1922 and 1923. Her mother's encroaching deafness curtailed Niedecker's college career; she returned home and cared for her mother until Daisy's death in 1951.

In 1925, Niedecker married Frank Hartwig, but the marriage lasted only a short time. Niedecker held a series of jobs. Among these were a library assistant at the Fort Atkinson Public Library and a proofreader for *Hoard's Dairyman* magazine. For a brief period, she worked for the WHA public radio station in Madison, where she wrote the scripts for radio plays, including an adaptation of William Faulkner's *As I Lay Dying*.

By 1931, some of Niedecker's poetry began appearing in magazines. She also began writing poet Louis Zukofsky. Influenced by the Objectivist Movement that flourished in the 1920s and 1930s, Niedecker sharpened her poetic skills until 1946, when she submitted a manuscript called *New Goose* to the James A. Decker Publishing Company.

The 1950s saw Niedecker in virtual seclusion on Black Hawk Island as she tried to cope with the deaths of both her parents within three years. She took up her father's renting out of the cabins to hunters and thus lived frugally for much of the decade. In 1957 she began work at the Fort Atkinson Memorial Hospital. All through the 1950s, Niedecker kept writing poetry and saw several of her works published in magazines, notably *Origins*, edited by Cid Corman. In 1961, she had a second book of poems published, *My Friend Tree*, by a small publisher in Scotland.

Niedecker married for a second time in 1964 to Al Millen. They lived in Milwaukee for a short time but returned to Fort Atkinson after Millen retired from business. She once commented that "he dotes on science fiction, but for me science seems more fictional than any story one could invent for it."

It wasn't until the late 1960s that Niedecker's poetry began to be recognized beyond her native Wisconsin. Within the short period from 1968 to 1970, three more books appeared: *North Central, T & G,* and *My Life By Water.*

On the last day of 1970, Niedecker died at her home on Black Hawk Island near Fort Atkinson. She was 67 years old.

Since her death, several more collections of her poetry have been published, including *Blue Chicory* (1976), *The Full Note* (1983), *The Granite Pail* (1985) and *Harpsichord & Salt Fish* (1991). *From This Condensery* was published in 1985.

Many of Niedecker's early poems are quite short. She exhibits a bit of Biercean macabre humor in a poem fragment about a woman choosing a dress to wear to a hanging — her own. "Will You Write Me A Christmas Poem?" reads much like T.S. Eliot's "The Wasteland" or "Ash Wednesday" with its repetitive lines denoting an almost stoical weariness mixed with Christian imagery and imaginative word play. Niedecker's poems are like little capsules that you pop into your mouth and they filter slowly toward your brain. All these fragmentary early poems show Niedecker searching for a proper language. Indeed, much of it does not read like poetry at all but simple mental jottings written on the spur of the moment.

"For Paul" is a series of poems written for Paul Zukofsky, the son of Louis Zukofsky with whom Niedecker had been corresponding since the 1930s. Niedecker seems at her best when singing the advent of nature.

While working at the Fort Atkinson Public Library,

Niedecker developed a keen awareness of the local history. She wrote several poems about area people including Thure Kumlein, also featured in Sterling North's books. Not without a biting sense of humor, Niedecker mixes in the same poem, Jesse and Frank James (the gunnin' Jameses) and William and Henry James (the writin' Jameses).

Another of Niedecker's early influences was the Japanese poet Basho and she tried her hand at haiku. But the Wisconsin landscape is forever at the forefront of Niedecker's poetry. She finds a deep juxtaposition between nature and mankind's effect upon it:

*North Central* features a series of poems about the early explorers of Wisconsin: Marquette, Radisson and Henry Rowe Schoolcraft, who passed this way and onward to find the source of the Mississippi River.

One of Niedecker's best long poems is "Wintergreen Ridge" which tells of the saving by a group of the townswomen of the so-named ridge from modern development. In *Harpsichord & Salt Fish* we find a long poem about Thomas Jefferson, one of many that Niedecker wrote concerning this founding father of America. Another excellent poem is "Subliminal", delving into the night world. There also is a long biographical poem about Charles Darwin and his voyages to the Galapagos Islands.

## LORINE NIEDECKER: SELECTED READING

• *From This Condensery: The Complete Writing of Lorine Niedecker,* edited by Robert J. Burnholt, 1985, The Jargon Society. 336 pp.

# EDNA MEUDT

Edna Meudt's grandparents came to America from Bohemia in 1871. They began farming in the Dodgeville area of Wisconsin because the land reminded them of what they had left behind in Europe.

In 1880, John Kritz, Edna's father, began working as a carpenter and handyman at the Hillside Home School. One of his co-workers was a young boy named Frank Lloyd Wright. Edna's mother was Kristine Nielsen, who came to America from Denmark in 1893. She met John Kritz in Milwaukee in 1899, married him, and they came to the farm in Wyoming Valley. When Edna was born in 1906, she was named Kristin Kritz and was looked after by an older brother, Leo.

Edna got polio in her first year and it wasn't until she was 3 that she could walk. When she was 3, Edna almost drowned in an accident where the wind blew the baby buggy she was in off the bridge near their farm and into the creek. In 1910, John Kritz grew gravely ill and Edna's mother was worried about the salvation of her child. So she had Kristin baptized and gave her a new name — Edna.

John Kritz eventually recovered from his illness, but Edna became quite susceptible to cold weather. In her early years she went to school at the one-room Kritz School where for three or four years she was the only student during the winter months. The Kritz farm stood just a couple of miles away from Frank Lloyd Wright's house, Taliesin. On August 15, 1914, Edna witnessed the fire that destroyed Taliesin and killed eight people. She would write of this event later in a poem called "A Summer Day That Changed The World."

When she was 14, Edna went to Madison to attend Edgewood Academy of the Sacred Heart, a boarding school run by Dominican sisters. It was a strict Catholic school and Edna shocked her tutors by exhibiting a knowledge of the works of Oscar Wilde, whose books were forbidden by

**Edna Meudt. Photo courtesy of Wisconsin Historical Society. (WHi-2652)**

the church.

Edna wasn't a very good student and sought other methods of expressing herself, including music and drama. Edna became engaged to a young man named Peter Meudt. It was practically an arranged engagement and marriage brought about by the parents. They were married shortly after Edna graduated from Edgewood in 1924. She soon had three children, one of whom died of a ruptured appendix at age 10. Edna settled down to life on a Wisconsin farm, and poetry was the furthest thing from her mind.

Sometime during the 1940s, Edna did take up the pen and started to write. At first she wrote fiction, but soon switched to poetry. In the early 1950s, she became involved with the fledgling Wisconsin Fellowship of Poets. She was its first secretary and later would twice serve as president.

Meudt's poetry came slowly. She was a tireless revisor and once she got involved in the numerous poetry societies that grew out of the Wisconsin Fellowship of Poets she was kept busy while still maintaining the farm on the outskirts of Dodgeville.

Her first book of poems was *Round River Canticle*, published by Wake-Brook House, a small specialty press originally based in Sanbornville, New Hampshire. In *Round River Canticle,* the early poems are more personal. Meudt speaks to a particular person in "Transition" and "Days of Grace."

"Elegy For A Priest" was written in memory of Father Daniel Coyne, a long-time spiritual friend of Edna's who died of a heart attack in 1959 while visiting Edna's home. Occasionally, Meudt uses images that are almost supernatural in effect, such as in the poem "Every Bridge We Crossed In Silence." A visit to a cemetery is reflected upon in "Part-Time Tenant" where the children run and play amongst the gravestones.

The first part of *Round River Canticle* is intensely religious as Meudt returns time after time to genuflect before the priest and friend who died. "The Woman Standing In The Midst" finds Meudt on the threshold of adulthood. "Made-To-Order Moons" contrasts the hurly-burly of modern civilization to the ancient land upon which Meudt lives. A simple poem is "Travelog," confessing her fear of heights, which never allows her the vision from above.

Meudt writes so often of childhood and family, yet her poems constantly surprise with a fresh phrase or timely insight. "The Round River Canticle" is Edna Meudt's paean to the life she has lived in Wisconsin: her life on the farm, close to nature and the passing of the years through marriage and children — but she always comes back to the land.

In 1964, *In No Strange Land* was published, also by Wake-Brook House. While the cloth covers of these books are attractive, the typeface of *In No Strange Land* is disappointing. The first few poems return to Edna's childhood. "First Journey" retells the story of taking her father to town at the onset of his illness. "Puccini and the Guest" concerns feeding a tramp in the kitchen with opera music in the background. "The Moldau at Our Door" finds the Kritzes taking in an injured German who later becomes a hired hand for the summer.

"Canticle For A Drummer Boy" is one of Meudt's longest poems. It segues nicely from a recapitulation of the life of the father of her priest friend Daniel Coyne who marched in the Civil War as a drummer boy to the modern festival that is Memorial Day.

Another long poem, broken into sections with epigrams

prefacing each section, is the title poem "In No Strange Land," which Meudt dedicates to her son Christopher. In the poem she experiences all the trials and joys of motherhood, finding the outside world large and frightening but knowing the inevitability of her child one day leaving to make his own place in it.

"Gossip Column" evokes the language of Iowa poet James Hearst as Edna watches a rooster caught amongst the hens. Her tone in this poem is wry and humorous. "Lamentation In Drought" carries the splendid image of "empty silos rear a new Carnac." Carnac is an ancient Druid megalithic site in England similar to Stonehenge.

More books followed: *No One Sings Face Down* was published in 1970 and five years later *The Ineluctable Sea* appeared, which contains a marvelous afterword by author Herbert Kubly touting Meudt's poetry as "at varying times lyric, nostalgic, elegiac and monumental." *The Ineluctable Sea* also chronicles a change in Meudt's poetry from the timeless to the more historically current. She often vents anger at the world of ignorance and violence she sees, such as in the poems "Sparrow in Church" and "A Ride In The Country." "Target Practice On Shining Mountain" ends with a beautiful phrase that flows like the wind it describes.

A large section of *The Ineluctable Sea* is devoted to August Derleth. Meudt chronicles in verdant prose the final three years of Derleth's life, through illness and the July 4th 1971, heart attack.

"Breakdown" chronicles Meudt's own "Dark Night Of The Soul," an analysis of doubt and looming despair.

In 1980, *Plain Chant For A Tree*, Meudt's fifth book of poems, was published by Wake-Brook House.

*The Rose Jar*, Edna Meudt's autobiography, was published by North Country Press in 1989, the same year that Edna Meudt died of natural causes at her home in Wyoming Valley. She was 83. In *The Rose Jar*, Edna included a lengthy section called "The Kristin Poems" which tells more of her childhood, including episodes where she kills her brother Leo's pet turtle and later kills a rattlesnake so she could get the bounty for the rattles and buy a shaving mug for her father's birthday. Another poem tells of a school teacher who died young. One of Edna Meudt's final poems, written when she was 79, is "Farm Woman."

**EDNA MEUDT: SELECTED READING**
- *Round River Canticle,* 1960, Wake-Brook House, Sanbornville, New Hampshire. 105 pp.
- *In No Strange Land,* 1964, Wake-Brook House, Coral Gables, Florida. 90 pp.
- *The Ineluctable Sea,* 1975, Wake-Brook House, Fort Lauderdale, Florida. 128 pp.
- *The Rose Jar: The Autobiography of Edna Meudt,* 1989, North Country Press, Madison, Wisconsin. 252 pp.

# KRISTINE KATHRYN RUSCH

It is Memorial Day weekend in Madison, Wisconsin. The year is 1993. At the downtown Concourse Hotel, a block away from the Capitol Square and the farmer's market, people flutter to and fro like displaced butterflies still wobbly after emerging from winter's cocoon. The event is WisCon, the world's foremost feminist science fiction convention. More than 500 science fiction fans, more than three-fourths of them women, are attending this year to pay tribute to the dual guests of honor. WisCon is a very intensive and scholarly convention—you won't see many Klingons or Wookies here— and this is its first year at the Concourse. In previous years, it was held in late March at a Holiday Inn southeast of the city.

Early in the convention one got the feeling that this was going to be a special WisCon. While Lois McMaster Bujold was genial and content to relax and bask in the glow of the the recent release of her Miles Vorkosigan novel *Cetaganda*, not so with the other guest of honor. Kristine Kathryn Rusch from the very first panel was a dynamo of intense concentration and resolve to bring forth the facts , the nuts and bolts of what it takes to become a professional writer, in particular a writer of science fiction, fantasy, and horror. In an hour-long workshop, I sat spellbound, watching Rusch surgically dissect and reconstruct the elements of a story. At this juncture of her life, Rusch was already the editor of *The Magazine of Fantasy & Science Fiction* and had published several fantasy novels. Her goliath publishing venture Pulphouse was about to dissolve due to the lack of time and money, but this wasn't about to stop her or even slow her down; she would simply shift gears.

By the end of WisCon, I had resolved to follow in Rusch's footsteps and become a full-time writer. Over the next seven months I wrote 38 short stories (many of which I would submit to Rusch at *Fantasy & Science Fiction*; none of which were accepted), well over one hundred poems, a couple of short novels and a half-dozen non-fiction articles. The fact that only a few of them sold and by the end of 1993 I was back in the working world seemed secondary to the accomplishment itself. Rusch has that effect on people.

So who is this woman who has almost single-handedly changed the world of fantasy and science-fiction? Both of Rusch's parents were born in Wisconsin. Her father, Carroll Rusch, was a college mathematics professor who, although tenured, moved from place to place. In 1960 he was teaching at Oneonta State Teacher's College in New York when Kristine was born on June 4th, the third of four children (two sisters and a brother). Carroll Rusch then moved to Fairfield, Iowa, where Kristine spent her early childhood as somewhat of a tomboy; a very athletic young girl who once suffered serious injuries in a bicycle accident. In 1967, Carroll Rusch moved again, this time to Superior, Wisconsin where he taught at the University of Wisconsin-Superior and had Arnold Schwartzenegger, who had enrolled as a math major, as a student.

Kristine was a gifted student. She attended McCaskill Lab School which was a teacher training grade school attached to the university. She was writing short stories and plays even before she was in junior high. Rusch later attended Superior Senior High School, where she found a kindred spirit in her English teacher, Virginia Kruse, who was the first person to encourage the teenager to become a professional writer.

After high school, Rusch attended Beloit College for one year, then transferred to the University of Wisconsin in Madison. She also married her high school sweetheart, but the marriage lasted just five years. At the University of Wisconsin, Rusch majored in history. She worked many jobs during college, including at William C. Brown Publishing Company and WORT radio, where she was the news director. She met Kevin J. Anderson, a fellow writer who would later co-write two novels with Rusch (*AfterImage* and

*AfterShock*). While in college she published a bit of non-fiction under the name Kristine K. Thompson.

In the late 1980s, Rusch had met Dean Wesley Smith and together they moved to Eugene, Oregon, where they created Pulphouse Publishing. It was an ambitious undertaking. Along with Debra Gray Cook, Mark Budz, Nina Kiriki Hoffman, Bill Trojan, and Phil Barnhart, the Pulphouse crew operated out of a warehouse outside of Eugene and produced not only a series of fine short novels in their acclaimed Axolotl Press series, but also put out a weekly fiction magazine and later *The Author's Choice Monthly*, a series of books featuring most of the outstanding science fiction and fantasy writers of the 1980s.

At the same time, Rusch was writing and selling short stories to professional markets. Her story "Sing" was the cover story for the March 1987 issue of *Aboriginal SF*, an Australian magazine. By 1988, she had hit her stride in the short story field with appearances in *Amazing Stories* ("Stained Black") and also *The Year's Best Science Fiction Anthology* ("Skin Deep"). The following year saw a real breakthrough with stories making the final ballot in both the science fiction (The Hugo Award) and horror (The Stoker Award) fields.

In 1991, Rusch cemented her reputation as one of science fiction and fantasy's rising young stars with the Axolotl Press Publication of her novella *The Gallery of His Dreams*. Previously published in Isaac Asimov's *Science Fiction Magazine,* this wonderful story won the Locus award for best novella and was a finalist for the Hugo award for best novella. It remains my favorite Rusch story and one of my all-time favorite stories.

*The Gallery of His Dreams* portrays young Mathew B. Brady through his later teenage years in New York City where he meets Samuel B. Morse (inventor of the telegraph) and signs up for a class in "image-making" using the recently patented daguerrotype — a forerunner of the modern camera. That night he has a dream about his future in which he meets a young woman in an art gallery. Nine years later, Brady meets his wife while dancing and she tells him of her dream — which is a replica of his: being in a gallery of his work, his photographs. The Civil War breaks out in 1861 and Brady is at the Battle of Bull Run. It is a weird scene as people, including Brady's wife, are picnicking on a hillside while the battle rages below. Then they are in the midst of it and Brady's viewpoint changes. His equipment is trampled and broken and he witnesses first hand the slaughter of innocents. The year 1863 finds Brady conscientiously at work on a Civil War battlefield, posing the dead bodies for his stark photographs. He turns to find a woman, vaguely familiar, standing beside him. She wants him to shoot pictures for her, offering to pay expenses. But before Brady can reply, she vanishes.

Brady is there at Appomattox to see the end of the war and takes a last photo of Robert E. Lee in Confederate uniform. But the acclaim is not there for Mathew Brady. He has traded everything he owns to continue his art. By 1871 he is broke, bankrupt, and with failing eyesight when the woman appears again. This time he takes her offer and is abruptly whisked to a war scene of utter horror somewhere in the Far East. Asian people are burning — but he must continue his work.

Again and again, Brady is sent to chronicle future scenes of horrific warfare: Vietnam, the Spanish Civil War and others. The strange woman explains that she has come from the future: Mathew Brady is her history project. And she continues to send him to places where death comes in inexplicable forms:

In *The Gallery of His Dreams*, Mathew Brady finally does get his exhibit, although to him the acclaim is for all the wrong reasons, but it somehow doesn't seem to matter now.

Later in 1991, Rusch accomplished two milestones. The first was publication of her first trade paperback novel, *The White Mists of Power,* a fantasy involving the struggles between two kingdoms. It was an impressive debut and the novel was highly praised. The second milestone was Rusch's being named th

e new editor at the prestigious *Magazine of Fantasy & Science Fiction*, replacing venerated founder Ed Ferman who had run the magazine for more than 25 years. At WisCon in 1993, Rusch told the story of how she had been given the manuscripts to a dozen stories submitted to the magazine and was told to go through them and select one that she would accept for publication. She did — and it was the same story that Ferman himself had selected.

Rusch had three books published in 1993: *Heart Readers* and *Traitors* were both in the fantasy vein, excellently written with tight and suspenseful plots. They show Rusch to be a fantasy writer of the first rank. The third novel, *Facade,* represented Rusch's foray into horror. In the early 1990s, the horror field had experienced a mild renaissance where the novels being written were full of sex and graphic violence: The term "cutting edge" was in vogue. *Facade* tried to follow in the same pattern, but it didn't work. The novel is relentlessly gloomy and tired. Rusch is not a horror writer. A second horror novel, *Sins of the Blood,* about a vampire brother and sister, though mildly interesting because of its Madison, Wisconsin, setting, is also a disappointment.

By 1996, Rusch had embarked upon a fantasy series, becoming ever more popular among fantasy writers. Although J.R.R. Tolkein had written his *Lord of the Rings* books, it wasn't until Terry Brooks in the late 1970s and then Robert Jordan in the early 1990s that fantasy series — an extensive series of books set in the same mythical land — captured the public imagination. Rusch began *The Fey*, a series of five books of fantasy which really captures her forte. These are exciting and memorable reads with real characters attempting to solve a multitude of problems.

The constant strain of her editorial duties with the *Magazine of Fantasy & Science Fiction* and her novel-writing had left Kris Rusch with little time to write short stories. In 1996, she had just one story published. And she had also begun (along with her husband Dean Wesley Smith) to contract for the writing of movie and media tie-in novelizations: *Star Trek* and *Aliens* being the most recognizable examples. It was with deep regret that Rusch resigned as editor (she had been the first female editor of a major science fiction magazine) of the *Magazine of Fantasy & Science Fiction*, but once that burden was lifted, she returned to short stories with a vengeance. In 1998, two of her stories, "Echea" and "Coolhunting," were nominated for Hugo awards.

"Echea" is a beautiful story about an Earth couple adopting a refugee child from the Moon. The couple travel to Sioux Falls — the nearest shuttle port — and return to their lakeside home in northern Wisconsin with Echea. The couple also have three daughters, and the youngest, Anne, adopts Echea as her play-pal. But Echea brings her own nightmares, and that disrupts the household. Since everyone is linked (e-mail is read on a screen inside the eyeball) Echea must undergo the linking procedure as well if she is to live a normal life on Earth. Then Echea's dark secret is revealed. She had been part of a prior project involving Moon children and already has an implant, but the Moon technology is incompatible with that of Earth. The only way to ensure Echea's status as a normal "human" is to remove the Moon implant which will unfortunately also remove all of Echea's memory of her previous life.

In "Coolhunting," a fashion hunter lives on the streets of New York City spotting the latest trends before they are popular. Then she gets a message that her sister is dying. Steffie returns to Michigan to see KD, a special child who has been kept at the age of 3 in physical form while her mind is older than Steffie's. A failed attempt with growth hormones has left KD at death's door. It is up to Steffie to take KD to a renegade doctor for a dangerous procedure, but the ending is not what one expects. As in so many of her stories, Rusch's deep empathy with the human situation and all its intangibles shines through the prose.

With her background in history, Rusch delved into a historical mystery in the thrilling novel *Hitler's Angel*. It tells the story of Adolf Hitler's secret love affair with his niece Geli Raubal and her mysterious death "by suicide," the investigation and aftermath of which may have prevented the Holocaust and World War II. Published in 1998, *Hitler's Angel* shows that Rusch is a fine mystery writer.

The year 2000 saw Rusch branch out into other fields of writing. As Kristine Grayson, she wrote a romance novel,

*Utterly Charming*, and later, *Thoroughly Kissed*. As Kris Nelscott, she wrote the mysteries *A Dangerous Road* and *Smoke-Filled Rooms*.

But it is fantasy that Rusch writes the best. She has begun another fantasy series, *The Black Throne*, and, as always, there are the wonderful short stories.

In 2000, Rusch's novella *Millennium Babies* won the Hugo Award in the novella category.

*Millennium Babies* is set in Madison, Wisconsin. Brooke Cross lives in a 150-year-old house with a real fireplace. She is contacted by a scientist, Eldon Franke, who wants to use her status as a Millennium Baby — she was born on January 1, 2000 — as part of a new study. Rusch unveils her familiarity with the University of Wisconsin campus, setting Brooke's office in Bascom Hall. Brooke now teaches history at the college. We learn that Brooke's birth was carefully planned by her mother so that she could be the first baby born in 2000 and thus earn for her mother a lot of money and prizes.

*Stories For An Enchanted Afternoon*, Rusch's first short story collection, was published by the Golden Gryphon Press in August of 2001. Included in this collection are "Echea", "Coolhunting," "Millennium Babies," "The Gallery of His Dreams" and seven more tales of science fiction and fantasy.

Living on a hilltop overlooking the Pacific Ocean in Eugene, Oregon, Rusch and her husband, Dean Wesley Smith, continue to weave marvelous tales of fantasy.

### KRISTINE KATHRYN RUSCH: SELECTED READING

- *The Gallery of his Dreams*, 1991, Axolotl Press, Pulphouse Publishing, Eugene, Oregon. 80 pp.
- *The White Mists of Power*, 1991, NAL/Roc, New York. 350 pp.
- *Heart Readers*, 1993, Penguin/Roc, New York. 287 pp.
- *Traitors*, 1994, Penguin/Roc, New York. 382 pp.
- *The Fey: The Sacrifice*, 1996, Bantam/Spectra, New York. 660 pp.
- *The Fey: The Changeling*, 1996, Bantam/Spectra, New

York. 606 pp.

• *Hitler's Angel,* 1998, St. Martin's Press, New York. 213 pp.

• *Stories for an Enchanted Afternoon,* 2001, Golden Gryphon Press, Urbana, Illinois. 284 pp.

• *Stained Black,* (audiocassette reading of the short stories "Stained Black", "Inspiration", "Fugue", and "Phantom"), 1990, Spine-Tingling Press, Agoura Hills, California. 3 hours.

# PETER STRAUB

Peter Straub mines almost exclusively in the caverns and open pits of horror. Straub's novels, from *Julia* to *Black House* (co-written with Stephen King), are excursions into the inner workings of the human mind, especially in regard to fear and terror. Next to his good friend King, Peter Straub is the finest writer of horror and suspense in the United States today.

Straub was born on March 2, 1943 in Milwaukee, Wisconsin. His early life was deeply influenced by the multicultural environs in which he was raised.

Peter early on became a voracious reader, gobbling up comic books then moving on to the Hardy Boys adventure stories by the time he was in fourth grade. He also had a period where he became an animal lover and read dog books (Alfred Payson Terhune), horse books, and stories about kid detectives. Mark Twain held his interest until sixth grade when he began reading science fiction. A.E. Van Vogt's *Slan* led him to read authors such as Isaac Asimov, Robert Heinlein, Frederick Pohl, and James Blish. His first glimpse of adult fiction came through the novels of Thomas Wolfe whom Straub first read at the age of 13.

When he was 7 years old, Peter was struck by a car and nearly killed. He spent months in a wheelchair and on crutches and this experience was transformed much later as part of another novel, *Koko*.

Straub's parents had different objectives for their son. His father wanted him to become a professional athlete while his mother preferred that he study for the priesthood. Straub would later incorporate the image of his father tossing baseballs to his inept son with increasing frustration into several autobiographical short stories.

In an interview with *Dark Echo Magazine*, Straub comments on what it was like to discover literature at such a young age:

"A proportionately very small number of children, mine

among them, grow up knowing writers, painters and musicians...but most children accept books, paintings, records as objects on the order of trees, rocks and rivers, elements of the landscape with no connection to human agency. When I was small, I knew that the books I read were *by* someone or other without quite grasping that a particular man or woman had taken the time to sit down and invent them. The name which followed *by* seemed eternal, remote, as impersonal as a granite inscription.

"At the same time, I really liked the idea and the act of writing."

Straub attended Milwaukee Country Day School on a scholarship, where he read Thomas Wolfe and Jack Kerouac and discovered jazz music. He also began writing stories.

He graduated from high school and enrolled at the University of Wisconsin in Madison where he earned a B.A. in English. Following his M.A. at Columbia University in New York City, Straub returned to Milwaukee and took a job teaching English literature at his old school, now renamed University School. In 1969, newly married, he moved to Dublin, Ireland, and fell in love with Dublin literary life. He met Thomas Tessier in Dublin and Tessier introduced him to the writings of H.P. Lovecraft, Robert Bloch, and Richard Matheson — all masters of horror. But Straub began by writing novels in the mainstream. He wrote *Marriages* while living in Dublin, and followed that up with an experimental novel called *Under Venus,* mostly set in the fictional Wisconsin town of Plechette City.

The year 1974 represented a watershed for Straub. His first horror novel, *Julia*, was published and instantly became a best-seller.

*Julia* begins with a young woman named Julia Lofting who has left her handsome, arrogant, womanizing husband Magnus after the tragic death of their only child, Kate. Buying a house on the outskirts of London, Julia sees a young girl who at first looks like the dead Kate. Later, Julia comes across the girl again in a park where the girl has just mutilated a turtle with a knife. We are given the story of Kate's death and Julia's subsequent hospitalization from which

Julia has recently been released. Kate had choked upon a piece of meat and Julia's husband, Magnus, had performed an unsuccessful tracheonomy.

A seance involving her husband's sister Lily's friends goes awry as the spectre manifests itself. Julia is again haunted by the cruel little blonde girl who beheads a wounded sparrow. Obsessed by her growing fascination with the haunted house, Julia researches its history and learns that a murder had taken place in the house some 20 years before — the murder of a young girl, Olivia Rudge, by her mother. It is Olivia's spirit that is haunting the house.

As in all good horror fiction, Straub's prose seamlessly carries the reader along to new heights of terror.

He followed up *Julia* with another story set in Wisconsin, *If You Could See Me Now*, about a man and a woman meeting again after 20 years at a place designated by their teenage selves. But horror lurks in the past of both people and it erupts and overwhelms the town of Arden.

*Ghost Story* appeared in 1979 and is Straub's affectionate nod to the old masters of the ghost story who appear as the names of the central characters in the Chowder Society. Four old storytellers share the dark secret of the murder of Eva Galli, a women each of them had known fifty years before. Now the ghost of Eva Galli (or Alma Mobley or Anna Mostyn) has reappeared seeking revenge. *Ghost Story* was made into an excellent movie starring Douglas Fairbanks Jr., Fred Astaire, Melvyn Douglas, and John Houseman as the Chowder Society and Alice Krige as the truly frightening and bewitching ghost.

*Shadowland* (1980) follows the adventures of two young boys apprenticed to a malevolent magician in the woods of Vermont. By now Straub had become a household name in the horror field and, in 1984, came a major work, *The Talisman*, co-authored with Stephen King. This tells the story of young Jack Sawyer, a 12-year-old boy whose actress mother Lily is dying of cancer. She is also fleeing Jack's late father's business partner Morgan Sloat, who is hounding her. On the beach at an Atlantic seacoast resort, Jack meets a handyman named Speedy who tells Jack of another world, the Territories, and of a dying queen of that world — who just may be his mother in this world. It is up to Jack to cross the country to fetch the object known as The Talisman in hopes of curing his mother, the queen, and saving both worlds. Morgan Sloat also knows of this world and tries to stop Jack. On his Galahadian quest, Jack meets with many adventures, both in this world and in The Territories. He finds his friend, Richard Sloat, who is Morgan's son, and despite Rational Richard's protests, drags him along into the Territories.

Some of the characters in *The Talisman* are unforgettable, particularly Wolf, Jack's werewolf friend who saves Jack's life from hell. There is also Sunlight Gardener, one of the creepiest villains this side of Hannibal Lecter.

Novel after novel flowed from Peter Straub's word processor: *The Throat, Mystery, The Hellfire Club, Koko* — each delivering its own brand of modern horror.

Although he rarely writes short stories, Straub also published two collections. *Houses Without Doors* appeared in 1990. It contains six stories that make up the essence of Peter Straub's early short fiction. "The Blue Rose" is a story about a young psychopath who hypnotizes his little brother. A sadist, he eventually causes young Eddie to die from an epileptic fit brought about while in a trance.

"The Juniper Tree" is a story involving a traumatic childhood incident where a young boy is sexually molested inside a movie theater. "A Short Guide to the City" is an interesting exploration of Milwaukee set against the backdrop of a serial killer who leaves the bodies of his victims beneath viaducts. Most fascinating are the descriptions of the Polish/Lithuanian communities and their customs and also the feral children of the ghetto.

"The Buffalo Hunter" involves a lonely man who makes up a dream life and tries to live by it. He has an obsession with baby bottles and nipples which allows him to drink his vodka in bed while reading books. *The Buffalo Hunter* is a western by Luke Short. Straub's main character, Bunting, suddenly finds himself inside the book, doing things the book does not describe. He becomes more and more desperate to stay inside the story permanently. But in a later novel, he finds the story intruding into his waking life. The prose here reads like a macabre, yet funny Robert Bloch story. But from *The Lady in the Lake* and Phillip Marlowe, Bunting turns to Anna Karenina.

"Mrs. God" is an eerie, slow-moving story about an American professor who travels to England to study a minor woman poet. Her past life is shrouded in mystery and a tragedy that involves Esswood House itself. It reads much like a cross between M.R. James and Nathaniel Hawthorne's *House of Seven Gables*.

*Magic Terror* is the most recent collection of Straub's short fiction. Its seven stories contain "Ashputtle" in which a fat woman schoolteacher hides a dark secret; "Isn't It Romantic?" is a bloody tale of murder and espionage in the Pyrenees Mountains between Spain and France. One of the best tales is "Porkpie Hat," a different kind of Straub story about a famous jazz musician and his past life.

"Mr. Clubb and Mr. Cuff" has a flavor of Herman Melville's "Bartleby the Scrivener" mixed in with Ambrose Bierce. A businessman hires two sadistic "consultants" to arrange the demise of his unfaithful wife and her lover. But Mr. Clubb and Mr. Cuff have their own way of doing things, which makes for a chilling unpleasantness, especially when it involves dental floss.

Seventeen years after *The Talisman*, Stephen King and Peter Straub hooked up again to produce *Black House*, the sequel about young Jack Sawyer, now 31 and recently retired from the Los Angeles Police Department. Jack wants to get away from the suddenly resurfacing memories of his past and travels to the coulee country of western Wisconsin, where he finds his dream refuge. *Black House* is a different sort of story from *The Talisman* and while the ending is slightly disappointing, it also sets up a possible third novel involving our hero Jack Sawyer.

Now splitting his time between New York City and England, Peter Straub continues to write excellent modern horror fiction.

### PETER STRAUB: SELECTED READING
- *Wild Animals: Three Novels: Julia, If You Could See Me Now, Under Venus,* 1984, G.P. Putnam's, New York. 591 pp.
- *Ghost Story,* 1980, Pocket Books, New York. 567 pp.
- *Shadowland,* 1981, Berkeley Books, New York. 468 pp.
- *The Talisman* (with Stephen King), 1984, Viking/Penguin, New York. 770 pp.
- *Houses Without Doors,* 1990, Dutton/Penguin, New York. 358 pp.
- *Magic Terror,* 2000, Random House, New York. 335 pp.
- *Black House* (with Stephen King), 2001, Random House, New York. 625 pp.

# JANE HAMILTON

One of the more recent female writers from Wisconsin to emerge on the national scene is Jane Hamilton. Three of her four novels were selected by Oprah Winfrey as part of her book club and as a result *The Book of Ruth, A Map Of The World,* and *Disobedience* became best sellers. Oprah Winfrey's influence, especially among women, is vast and undeniable. Ironically, *The Book of Ruth* had been in print for nearly a decade before Winfrey's selection sent it onto the best-seller list.

Jane Hamilton is as down-to-earth as one can get, as a writer and a person. She was born in 1957 in Oak Park, Illinois. Her mother was a poet and journalist and her father was an omnivorous book reader. Her grandmother wrote novels that were never published. As a young girl, Jane studied dance and uses much of her knowledge in *The Short History of A Prince.* She grew up reading the Victorian novelists: Dickens, George Eliot, Tolstoy and others. She graduated from Carleton College in Minnesota in 1979 with an English degree. Never accepted into a graduate level writing course, Jane wrote in her spare time. Her first novel, *The Book of Ruth,* took three years to write and got a lot of rejections before it sold.

*The Book of Ruth* begins in Honey Creek, Illinois, a town so small that when they hold a parade, there's no one to cheer because everybody's in the parade. Hamilton's easy prose style hearkens to the days of Zona Gale or Eudora Welty. Ruth is a young girl growing up on a rural farm. Ruth's mother, May, married a young farmer who was killed in World War II. May spent a long time getting over his death before she remarried.

Hamilton enjoys giving the reader scenes of common, everyday life. While some reviewers called *The Book of Ruth* Dickensian in style, while reading of Ruby's past life and all the incidents between Ruby and May, I kept thinking more of the short stories of William Faulkner or the novels of

**Jane Hamilton. Photo by Mark Hertzberg of the** *Racine Journal Times.*

John Steinbeck.

Ruth gets pregnant, which places an added burden on May and Ruby. The baby arrives and they call the boy Justin Dahl. This is a fine novel and while one tends to become impatient with Ruth at times, there's always an awareness of the fact that she is doing the best that she can.

Hamilton's next book was *A Map Of The World,* published

in 1994. Alice Goodwin is a hard-working rural farm wife and mother to two daughters, Claire and Emma. Her husband, Howard, is busy with the dairy farm, the only one left in an area surrounded by subdivisions. One day Alice, while rummaging in the attic for a swimming suit, discovers a map of the world — an imaginary world she called Tangalooponda — which she created at the age of nine, spending months drawing the towns and hills and rivers and people. While Alice is looking at the map, Lizzy, a neighbor's two-year-old daughter whom Alice had been baby-sitting, falls into the pond behind the house and drowns.

One of the most heart-rendering and poignant scenes in *A Map Of The World* comes when Howard and Teresa finally let the dam of their long-pent emotions burst. They comfort each other on the porch of Howard's house while the children sleep inside.

*The Short History Of A Prince* was published in 1998. In an interview, Hamilton said that it normally takes her about three years to write a novel start to finish. She is constantly revising it and inserting lines here and there. The effort shows in the gracefulness of her prose.

Walter McCloud, the leading character, was influenced at an early age by his aunt. Later, Walter reflects upon the present and past, and the novel shifts time frames back and forth to present these episodes.

One of the more amusing chapters in the book describes Walter's life as an English teacher in the small town of Otten, Wisconsin. Day after day he tries to spark a flame of interest in his students. Hamilton here paints a realistic portrayal of the difficulties the high school English teacher faces in his daily life.

We are gradually given glimpses of Walter's homosexuality. He has taken up with a lover in Chicago after a series of short-lived episodes with other men. A memorable scene is Walter dressing in the costume of the girl who is playing Odile, the evil swan in Swan Lake.

The final chapters in *The Short History Of A Prince* deal with Walter's older brother Daniel, who died at 18 of

Hodgkin's Disease. Over 20 years later, Daniel's death provides the means of redemption for the McCloud family to save their ancestral home on Lake Margaret.

*Disobedience* was published in 2000. The novel follows 17-year-old Henry Shaw as he unwittingly downloads his mother's e-mail from the computer and learns of her illicit love affair with another man.

Hamilton throws in loopy metaphors, such as calling English morris dancing "the pagan precursors to the aerobic worship of the body, minus the spandex and the hand weights." She realistically depicts the mental doubt and anguish that courses through young Henry's head as he realizes the seriousness of his mother's extramarital relationship.

At times Hamilton captures the grace of life in prose so vibrant that you can almost feel yourself a part of the scene.

There are many quirky aspects that make Hamilton's novels stand out from her Wisconsin contemporaries. Her characters all seem to have a solid background in literature and music. It is often these qualities that allow them to survive the situations in which she places them. Each story develops at a natural pace with just enough substance to keep the reader interested. Current events often are inserted, lending a verisimilitude to the narrative. Many locales are familiar to Wisconsin readers and she refers to the homes of the primary characters by their house numbers.

From her orchard farmhouse near Rochester, Wisconsin, Jane Hamilton continues to write.

### JANE HAMILTON: SELECTED READING

- *The Book of Ruth*, 1988, Anchor Books/Doubleday, New York. 328 pp.
- *A Map of the World*, 1994, Doubleday, New York. 390 pp.
- *The Short History of a Prince*, 1998, Random House, New York. 349 pp
- *Disobedience*, 2000, Doubleday, New York. 273 pp.

# BEN LOGAN

Ben Logan was born in 1920 on a country farm in the Kickapoo River valley about nine miles from where the Kickapoo joins the Mississippi River. He was the youngest of four brothers and his childhood as recounted in *The Land Remembers* was basically idyllic. The Depression did not ravage the Kickapoo Valley to the extent it did in urban areas. The exposure he did get usually came from the itinerant hired men who came to work the fall harvest for a few weeks.

**Ben Logan. Photo courtesy of the *Wisconsin State Journal/ Capital Times* newsroom library.**

Logan went to the University of Wisconsin, but soon transferred to New York University. During World War II, he was stationed in the Mediterranean supervising landing craft. After the war, he resumed studies at the University of the Americas. A later period found him living in Mexico for several years where he became interested in anthropology and pre-Columbian history. He returned to New York and spent many years writing for radio and television.

In the early 1990s, Logan returned to Wisconsin, living on the old family farm near Gays Mills. His most recent book is *Christmas Remembered,* published by Northword Press and a story from that book appeared in the December 1999 issue of *Viroqua Sights & Sounds* magazine.

*The Land Remembers* is broken into five parts, beginning with a "Genesis," which asks the question of how to tell the story of a farm. Here, he breaks it down into four seasons and each has its own parcel of stories to tell.

Spring is the season of growing and the titles of each chapter reflect that, including: "The Awakening Land," "The Magic Seeds," "The Garden" and "Black Grass," which tells of the firing of the prairie, burning off last summer's old growth to bring about new growth.

Summer is "A Place for Dreams." It is the longest section and gives sharp images of what summer was like on a farm — from the bone-aching days of haying to restless rainy days to hunting for bee trees. Also in late summer would come the hired men, mostly hoboes in those Depression days, riding the rails and looking for enough work to fill their pockets with food, money being a scarce commodity.

Fall was "A Time of Change." School beckoned, the corn harvest, and the arrival of the first killing frost. Yet for all of that, fall was a favorite time of the year.

Winter meant staying close to the house and barn — and the neighbor's corn shredder, which had broken down and stayed at the farm all winter long. Winter also meant raging blizzards, the joys of sledding and the Christmas season, which brings hope of a prosperous New Year.

Ben Logan's other well-known book is *The Empty Meadow.* It tells the story of Steve Carlson, a 17-year-old farm boy who listens to the older men sitting around the bars and general stores in a 1930s Wisconsin town. The stories he hears about men and women bring his own desires into sharp conflict. He attends Saturday night dances with his friend Billy Wallin and meets up with the daughter of a clammer who lives in a tarpaper shack along the Mississippi River while her father dredges for clams.

Steve learns the social differences that exist between the townsfolk and those who live along the river. He loses the clammer's daughter, but soon finds Elaine, who is strong-willed, but not ready for a relationship. Steve gets advice on women from Bottles, an alcoholic poet- philosopher who quotes Shakespeare, Michelangelo, and even Thoreau's Walden. Steve also befriends "The Oldest Man in the World" — Billy Wallin's 96-year-old great-grandfather.

The course of events takes place during one long, hot summer and the focus is almost entirely on Steve. The book has numerous moments of humor, including a late night "cow rodeo" that goes awry.

### BEN LOGAN: SELECTED READING

• *The Land Remembers,* 1992, Heartland Press, 25th anniversary commemorative edition, 192 pp.

• *The Empty Meadow,* 1983, Stanton & Lee, Madison, WI, 221 pp.

# LORRIE MOORE

When Lorrie Moore's *Birds of America* was published in 1999 it quickly became widely popular and appeared on the *New York Times* best seller list. Not many short story collections make best sellers and even fewer are collections of mainstream stories.

Since 1984, Lorrie Moore has taught English at the University of Wisconsin in Madison and all of her published works have come during this time, but her roots began elsewhere.

She was born Lorena Marie Moore in 1957. Nicknamed Lorrie, she grew up in Glens Falls, New York, the second of four children. Her father was an insurance agent, her mother a nurse turned housewife. As a child, Moore was a quiet and skinny kid. She often fretted, quite literally, about her thinness. "I felt completely shy, and so completely thin that I was afraid to walk over grates. I thought I would fall through them."

Moore began writing as a teenager and her first submission won a short story contest for *Seventeen* magazine. She got a $500 prize.

Moore attended St. Lawrence University and after graduation moved to Manhattan where she found work as a paralegal. At this time Moore also enrolled at Cornell University. Her first novel, *Self-Help,* was written while in the M.F.A. Program in English at Cornell. An accomplished pianist, Moore gave up a possible career as a musician to concentrate on her writing.

*Self-Help* shows early on the promise that Moore held as a writer. It is extremely self-conscious in places, which reflects an attitude much in vogue with writers in the 1980s.

"How To Be An Other Woman" is fragmentary, disjointed, an amalgam of crudely created scenes. "What Is Seized" is much better, an autobiographical story about childhood and is grimly realistic in depicting the parents. It ends with a woman coming to terms with her mother's death.

"How" is about the break-up of a relationship. "Go Like This" depicts a woman diagnosed with cancer who calmly goes about planning her suicide. "How To Talk To Your Mother (Notes)" chronicles in reverse order from the death of her mother to her own birth, year-by- year, in little snippets. "Amahl and The Night Visitors" is about a dependent woman who tries to cling to her relationship with an actor.

"How To Become A Writer" is quite bitter and amusing. "To Fill" becomes a depressing story about a woman slowly going mad with anxiety about her weight and her already mad mother.

All told, in this first book by Lorrie Moore, there is no *Self-Help*.

Moore continued to write short stories and they were published in *GQ*, *The New Yorker,* and *The Tampa Review.* In 1990, her second collection, *Life Like,* appeared. These stories show that Moore has sharpened her perception and skill at portraying the tiny unusual moments in modern life. "Two Boys" finds Mary divided between the two young men in her life. One offers security, the other risk and excitement.

"Vissi D'Arte" is about a playwright living in a seedy area of New York. "Joy" is about a woman alone with a cat and a dead-end job. "You're Ugly, Too" finds Zoe, another woman trapped in a loveless life, afraid of herself and of men. Several of Moore's stories end with a random act of violence, usually by women toward men.

"Places To Look For Your Mind" is a rather charming, slightly dotty story about two New York parents, themselves not entirely of this world, who take in an English visitor, a friend of their daughter who is living overseas. For three days he roams New York and you think something's going to happen but no, one day he's just gone — to Los Angeles and then back to England.

"Life Like," the title story, carries the reader along with a sense of mystery and is an enjoyable read.

*Who Will Run The Frog Hospital?* appeared in 1994. Moore has turned her penchant for witty humor to good use in this story of two girls growing up.

**A 1994 photo of Lorrie Moore. Photo courtesy of *Wisconsin State Journal/Capital Times* newsroom library.**

Berie and Sils are 15-year-old girls who spend a summer working at Storyland, an amusement park in upstate New York. While with some boys who had a BB gun, Berie watches them shoot frogs in a nearby marsh. Later, she and Sils try to save the wounded frogs and Sils creates a painting of the two and the frogs which she called "Who Will Run The Frog Hospital?" Moore realistically captures the simultaneous excitement and tedium of teenage girlhood.

*Anagrams* was published in 1997. It's a tale about Benna and Gerard, who first live in adjoining apartments but later move in together. Gerard is moody and creative. Benna teaches poetry (badly) at a local junior college. They each see other people while trying to establish a relationship.

Gerard and Benna split up and hold a yard sale with Benna's friend Eleanor. It's a funny, wretched scene as all three struggle to mask their thoughts from each other.

Moore shifts time frames, looping back and forth to spotlight certain events in both Benna's and Gerard's lives. At times *Anagrams* gives off a Lewis Carroll Alice-in-Wonderland feel which leaves a less attentive reader foundering.

*Birds of America* finds Moore back to the short story form.

In "Willing," Sidhra is a former movie actress, now turning forty, who is too aware that her life has changed, become formless. "Which Is More Than I Can Say About Some People" finds a woman and her mother travelling to Ireland to kiss the Blarney Stone. She goes through a series of misadventures, including going to the bathroom behind a stone fence in full view of a dozen black sheep.

Kissing the Blarney Stone proves to be a thoroughly unsettling experience as both women fall prey to doubts and insecurities...both of the Stone and of themselves. But it's this experience that bonds the two women together as nothing had before. A nice little story with an upbeat ending.

"Dance in America" is a moving, believable story about a woman dancer who meets up with an old flame who has a seven-year-old son with cystic fibrosis. They stay up late one night dancing to a Kenny Loggins song, making one more joyous memory for the boy to take to the grave.

There is something about Moore's style that draws you in, like tugging on a string to capture the attention of a cat, then jerking it away just as the cat snatches at it. In "Community Life," Olena is a Romanian immigrant who moves to an unnamed midwestern city (based on Madison), gets a job in the library and takes up with a reformed anarchist who had once bombed a campus building. She tries to get involved with Nick's campaigning for a local politician, but when he sleeps with another woman, Olena feels abandoned. "Alone as a book, alone as a desk, alone as a library, alone as a pencil, alone as a catalog, alone as a number, alone as a notepad.

"Agnes of Iowa" is a story in which even when Moore's female characters try to break out of the cycle of an aimless, meaningless life, something crops up to put them back into their place. Agnes teaches a night class in writing at the university and falls victim to university politics. When she meets a visiting South African poet and discovers that her preconceptions are false and she develops an interest in him, he goes off and she's left alone again in a failing marriage.

In another story, a woman tries to get over the death of her beloved cat. Psychotherapy fails to the tune of thousands of dollars. In "Beautiful Grade" Moore describes a smile as "like something brief and floral and in need of heat."

One of the more remarkable stories in *Birds of America* is "Real Estate," the story of a marriage spinning out of control that is Moore's darkest and funniest story. In "People Like That Are The Only People Here," Moore takes a vibrant and personal look at one woman's fears and anger when her child is diagnosed with cancer. As she spends an entire weekend in the hospital, both before and after the surgery, we are given a no-nonsense account of what goes through the human mind—both male and female—at times of crisis.

"Terrific Mother" finds a woman and her husband at a villa in Italy, surrounded by academics. She is trying to live with herself after causing the accidental death of a neighbor's baby whom she had been holding. The woman is helped by a Swedish masseuse from Minnesota, but the sessions turn out to be more than what she had expected.

Lorrie Moore is at the height of her writing career. She's still teaching at the University of Wisconsin in Madison and it will be interesting to see where she goes next in her books.

**LORRIE MOORE: SELECTED READING**
- *Self-Help,* 1985. Alfred Knopf, New York. 163 pp.
- *Like Life*, 1990. Alfred Knopf, New York. 178 pp.
- *Who Will Run the Frog Hospital?* 1994. Alfred Knopf, New York. 148 pp.
- *Anagrams,* 1997. Alfred Knopf, New York. 229 pp.
- *Birds of America,* 1999. Alfred Knopf, New York. 291 pp.

# WILLIAM F. STEUBER

William F. Steuber was born in 1904 in Prairie du Sac, Wisconsin. He went to the University of Wisconsin in Madison and graduated with an engineering degree. Much of his life was spent working with the state government, involving highways, natural resources, public information, history, and Indians.

He came to fiction writing late in life. His first book, *The Landlooker,* was published when he was 53. He published another novel, *Us, Incorporated* in 1963 and followed that with *Go Away, Thunder* in 1972. Steuber currently lives in Madison.

*The Landlooker* tells the story of Emil Rohland, the youngest son of a famous Chicago harness-making family. The year is 1871 and the Rohlands want to expand their business. So young Emil, who is 15, and his older brother Rudolph are sent out into the wilds of Wisconsin to look for other markets for harnesses.

Pa Rohland has bought back from the government three train car loads of surplus Civil War harnesses that the Rohlands had made. Rudolph is full of wild plans about making big deals while Emil is sent to sell harnesses at the outlying farms.

They visit North Woods logging camps where the rough, boisterous life and sudden deaths give Emil a new perspective on his own existence. He is accidentally taken on a wild ride on a log raft through the Wisconsin River rapids; Rudolph becomes sick through excessive drinking and gambling; and, as is invariably found in Wisconsin novels and accounts of the period, there is a scene of the slaughter of the passenger pigeons.

Emil and Rudolph arrive in Peshtigo on the eve of the Great Fire. While back in Chicago, Rudolph had seduced a servant girl named Sarah and abandoned her to go on this trip. Sarah has returned to her native Peshtigo, carrying

**William F. Steuber. Photo courtesy of** *Wisconsin State Journal/Capital Times* **newsroom library.**

Rudolph's child. Emil meets Sarah just as the fire threatens the town. This is some of the most harrowing writing in Wisconsin literature as Steuber describes the plight of Emil and Sarah attempting to make their way through the incendiary holocaust to the river where Sarah's baby is born while she stands in the water.

*Go Away, Thunder* is a novel of the Menomonie Indians circa the 1200s in Wisconsin. Kimewan, a young woman, is in love with Two Bears, a strong warrior and hunter. Two Bears loves her, but on the night of the wild rice dance, Kimewan gets her period and must be secluded in her hut, so Two Bears must wait. Finally, he enters her house as her parents sleep.

She is not there, having gone to gather herbs and roots to make a love potion. When she returns, Two Bears is still there, and by morning they have become man and wife. Two Bears has a friend, Low Red Moon, who is more of a thinker. They hatch a plan to win a lacrosse game against the neighboring Ojibwa. But the plan goes wrong and Low

Red Moon is shamed.

Another character is Chipmunk, who fears thunder. When he goes away to fast and receive his vision, he manufactures a false story, bringing with him a lightning-struck branch which he rips apart with his bare hands, no one else having seen the tiny crack that had already weakened the wood.

### WILLIAM F. STEUBER: SELECTED READING
- *Go Away, Thunder,* 1972, Wisconsin House, 172 pp.
- *The Landlooker,* 1957, 1991, Prairie Oak Press, Madison, WI, 367 pp.

# KELLY CHERRY

Kelly Cherry can be considered the spearpoint of modern Wisconsin female writers. Her first writings were published at the height of the feminist movement in the 1960s and 1970s. Today, Cherry continues to explore the role of women in modern society in her fiction, poetry and non-fiction essays.

Cherry was born in 1946 in Louisiana. As a child, her neighbors called her a "child of nature" for her wild, unkempt look. Her parents were musicians and often let Cherry run free. In college, she was a vagabond, attending five different schools, including the New Mexico Institute of Mining and Technology, but she preferred the study of philosophy. When she was 19, she went to Russia, where she met a Latvian composer named Imants Kalnin. Their story is told in *The Exiled Heart: A Meditative Autobiography*.

It was while she was at the University of Virginia that Cherry developed an interest in writing. She and a few other students, including Henry Taylor and Richard Dillard, would meet at night in an empty classroom to share and critique each other's writings. They called themselves the Bootleg Poetry Seminar. She would spend the next few years living in New York, writing and struggling through a short-lived marriage.

Cherry began teaching at the University of Wisconsin in Madison in 1980, where she was later named to the Eudora Welty Chair of English and taught creative writing to many of today's young writers.

Her first book was a novel, *Sick and Full of Burning*, published in 1974. In the novel's opening segment, "The Angel of Explanation," Mary "Tennessee" Settleworth is a 30-year-old woman who takes a job as a governess to a 14-year-old rock music freak named Cammie Carlisle. Once Cammie leaves to attend another school, Tennessee stays on with Cammie's mother, Lulu, and the housemaid, Willa Mae

Wood, a huge black woman full of lust and life. Tennessee becomes part of a feminist group and attends their meetings where she finds conflict. She meets Adrien, who flits in and out of her life throughout the book, a friend not willing to become a lover.

"The Black-and-Blues" finds Tennessee desperate for sex — to the point of turning off her first obscene phone caller and turning on a vibrator. She enrolls in a class in gynecology at Mount Sinai Medical School in New York where she tries to overcome the prevalent assumption that men make the best gynecologists.

Some of the best parts in the book are the encounters between Tennessee and the other four women in her feminist group. Cherry inserts these episodes at appropriate breaks in the novel's flow in order to make or reinforce a point or analyze a situation. One woman in the group constantly weeps, another takes a tough, aggressive stance and Tennessee is torn between the "trends" of the era and her own desire for a man.

Cherry's first book of poetry was published in 1975 by Red Clay Press of Charlotte, North Carolina. *Lovers & Agnostics* had a limited printing and is representative of Cherry's early work. In 1977 came another book of poems, *Relativity: A Point of View*. It begins with a lovely poem about the first woman to orbit the earth, Valentina Vladimirovna Tereshkova.

Cherry poses riddles and gives answers; her poem on Joan of Arc is short and sweet and full of fire. "Sequence Sonnet" is an amusing poem about what a woman in love will plan to trap a man, everything from Beethoven to bouquets. Cherry exhibits a wicked bite in poems regarding love. She pens a parody of Marvell's "To His Coy Mistress," who in this take is decidedly uncoy! Archaeological imagery suffuses many of Cherry's poems in this collection.

Cherry ends this book with a long poem called "A Bird's-Eye View Of Einstein." The poem is replete with startling imagery and language. It weaves science and mythology, the memories of childhood, the lost brother, the suffering Christ father, and vindication of the path chosen in life.

**Kelly Cherry. Photo by Meg Theno, courtesy of *Wisconsin State Journal/Capital Times* newsroom library.**

*Augusta Played*, published in 1979, finds Cherry turning toward humor and irony in her work. This novel depicts Augusta "Gus," a promising young flutist who shares the world with her canary and a strange melange of other characters—from her distrustful husband to an absent-minded professor to a stripper and a peeping-tom bellboy.

Also published in 1979 was a novella, *Conversion*, about a woman who has troubles in her relationships with men. Early in the story there's a wonderful exchange between the woman and her at-the-time lover.

Cherry would return to and expand upon a form of mad-cap situational humor in her next novel, *In The Wink Of An Eye.* The story begins with Miguel and Ramon, two Bolivian revolutionaries hiding out in the Bolivian jungle after pulling off a bank robbery which netted them three million dollars. *In The Wink Of An Eye* is a fine book, full of wit and humor and memorable characters.

*The Lost Traveller's Dream* (1984) appears to be part of several of Cherry's earlier works knitted together into an experimental novel.

Early on, Cherry again mentions the incidents with the Latvian composer from *The Exiled Heart.* Since the copyright is dated 1971, one wonders if Cherry inserted this passage later. *The Lost Traveller's Dream* is a young person's novel that captures society as it was in the early 1970s. A woman who has just been divorced finds another lover in her husband's brother and they go "bombing" around. Marijuana is smoked frequently and its effects are analyzed. Later, she meets with a rabbi and tries to seduce him.

The relationship between Cherry's female protagonist, Katie Allen, and the hedonistic rabbi taunts and teases in erotic overtones. Yet one can't help but feel exasperated at their constant evasions.

*Natural Theology*, a collection of poems, appeared in 1988 and *My Life and Dr. Joyce Brothers,* published in 1990, was an unexpected best-seller. It is a novel set in stories about aging, disease, marriage, and sexual relationships.

*The Exiled Heart: A Meditative Autobiography,* published in 1991, recounts Cherry's romance and near marriage to the well-known Latvian composer Imants Kalnin. Cherry met Imants in Moscow in 1965 and they spent four days together, long enough to fall in love. Cherry returned to Latvia to see Imants, but this time she finds obstacles thrown in their way by the Soviet government. By 1975 Cherry was willing to leave America and live with Imants in Latvia and she tries to comply with all the regulations, but to no avail. The Soviet system is suspicious of her motives and refuses permission. Just before leaving Latvia for the second time, Cherry reflects on the freedoms that Americans take for granted.

*God's Loud Hand*, a collection of poetry, appeared in 1993. It is full of images of Christ: seated on a crested wave, tired from his journey walking on the waters (Galilee); Christ in the Garden of Gethsemane surrounded by sleeping apostles.

One of my favorite poems in this collection is "Song of the Siberian Shaman." In "At A Russian Writers' Colony," the words are black with the stain of cigarettes. They burn like bones in a crematorium and we sift through the ashes looking for something to salvage. "Passing People on the Street" gives us a glimpse of the last years of life in slowly crumbling bodies. Splendid imagery, haunting and harrowed. Cherry ends this collection with a brilliant sestina "God's Friends Will Wear Rain*Bows."

*Writing the World* is a collection of essays published in 1995. In the essay "On Wisconsin," Cherry talks much about the nature of writing. In "The Place Where There Is Writing," she describes a visit to the ancient Mayan ruins at Dzibilchaltun on the Yucatan peninsula. While she was there, a rainstorm blew over, leaving her all alone on top of the ruin. Cherry felt a oneness with the place until she wished that she could read the writing of the rain as it fell upon the rocks.

Cherry's 1999 book, *The Society of Friends,* is a short story collection. Set in Madison, these stories feature the neighbors, colleagues and acquaintances of Nina Bryant. Nina is a writer and university professor and, as each story develops, it tells the tales of people trying to live according to their principles. Mystery surrounds each individual's life, be they an independent bookstore owner, a high school language teacher, a nurse, or a commodities broker. Cherry takes an honest look at all the dark strings that tug at the human heart.

In May of 2000, Kelly Cherry resigned her post as the Eudora Welty Chair of English and later filed suit against the university, charging sex discrimination in the rate of pay between male and female faculty members. She left

Madison and moved to Halifax, Virginia, with her husband and two dogs.

### KELLY CHERRY: SELECTED READING

- *Sick and Full of Burning,* 1974, Viking Press, New York. 280 pp.
- *Relativity: A Point of View,* 1977, Louisiana State University Press, Baton Rouge. 59 pp.
- *Conversion,* 1979, Treacle Press, New York. 45 pp.
- *In the Wink of an Eye,* 1983, Harcourt, Brace, Jovanovich, New York. 305 pp.
- *The Lost Traveller's Dream,* 1984, Harcourt, Brace, Jovanovich, New York. 231 pp.
- *The Exiled Heart: A Meditative Autobiography,* 1990, Louisiana State University Press, Baton Rouge. 268 pp.
- *God's Loud Hand,* 1993, Louisiana State University Press, Baton Rouge. 58 pp.
- *Writing the World,* 1995, University of Missouri Press, Columbia. 147 pp.
- *The Society of Friends,* 1999, University of Missouri Press. 228 pp.

# NORBERT BLEI

Norbert Blei has a way with words. Words that capture the essence of things, of feelings, of awareness of the visible and the invisible. He is an interior writer, working out a necessary salvation by use of wordcraft. He feels the shape of existence, both his own and that of others. He describes with an intensity utterly human and involved. He mingles and mixes with the flow, sometimes quiescent,

**Norbert Blei. Photo courtesy of _Wisconsin State Journal/Capital Times_ newsroom library.**

sometimes bullying (or perhaps "badgering") until the form he desires is just right. He is a writer of our times.

Norbert Blei was born in Chicago and did not come to Wisconsin until the late 1960s. He made Wisconsin's Door County his own private Walden Pond, but rather than holding back and observing, Blei plunged right into the realities of everyday life in such a rural setting. He continues to live in Ellison Bay but spends much time in New Mexico, among other places.

_The Hour of the Sunshine Now_ is Blei's second book, following _The Watercolor Way_ (1969). It is a short story collection, the first part of which uses Blei's memories of childhood in an ethnic Slavic neighborhood in Chicago. The last story is a true gem, portraying the life of a woman painter who seeks and finds salvation in its truest biblical sense in the New Mexico desert. Each segment of this tale is prefaced with the title of a Paul Klee painting. Another good story is "A Distance of Horses," about a teacher who has in his class in northern Wisconsin, a young Arab man who cannot find expression of himself in the English language, but whose failed attempt at capturing the beauty of a horse finds a spark inside the teacher.

*Door Way,* subtitled "The People in the Landscape," is a charming and thoughtful book, an account of the lives of several people — many from the Chicago area — who have made Door County their home. Along with a few, like the dancer, Karen, a bird of passage who uses movement to express herself, Blei profiles a broad mix — everyone from ministers and painters to migrants and horse traders. In many chapters Blei notes the changes, the influx of modern ways into the Door County landscape. Often he laments these changes, but ultimately realizes the inevitability of what is occurring.

One of his best — and shortest — essays is "Death of a Country Road." He sees the trees brought down and the old gravel paved over in asphalt or concrete. Each character is true to life, some are saints and some are sinners, but all are real and all are human. Interestingly, although politics is frequently used to bring about the changes in Door County that Blei decries, few of the figures he portrays have political savvy or know-how. More frequent are the poets, philosophers and artisans who find in the Door landscape an extension of their own inner feelings and struggles.

Blei followed *Door Way* two years later with *Door Steps.* The first part of this book is a day-journal that Blei kept, mostly an internal monologue noting and describing the daily events at his Door County chicken coop which he turned into his own studio. A nice example is this entry for July 19:

"Web Light: A morning of magic, of fantasy, of fairy tale, a sunny summer morning of heavy dew, a morning I witness perhaps once a year, though years may pass when I fail to find such a fine magic to the day at all. A thin morning, a morning of webs. The dew must be present... and the sun, at such an angle, and the time of day so precise (after

6 a.m.?) that the delicacy of the moment (light and dew) can easily dissipate before one's eyes. But they are there now... here in the fold... thousands of them surround me, my shoes and pantlegs wet with dew. The magic, the mystery, the secrecy of spiderwebs set so surely in the private places of the weeds and flowered fields... The webs spin in their own light like ghosts of flowers." (p. 98)

Other sections of *Door Steps* include: "The Seasons" which recounts "Visiting Door in Winter," "Waiting for Spring in Door County," "Summer Gone" and "The Season of Looking Back." Blei's well-known essay "Christmas Eve in Door" completes the book. In "Summer Gone," Blei paints a humorous and accurate picture of the tourist season, cars jammed bumper-to-bumper for miles along the two main arteries through Door County.

Blei's final book in the trilogy, *Door to Door,* is very similar to *Door Way.* He includes essays on The Clearing, where he has taught writing workshops for nearly two decades; painting by watercolor, as an extension of his first novel; a trip to see Illinois poet Dave Etter; and more profiles of the people of Door County.

Along with his Door County books, Blei has continued to write fiction. Another collection of his stories, *The Ghost of Sandburg's Phizzog,* resumes his honest and often pitiless look at the human condition. In "Skarda," the visit of an old gypsy woman leaves a young boy puzzled by mysteries he does not understand. Other stories include a middle-aged landlord who has an affair with a married female tenant; a grim story of a Vietnam vet going to a legion meeting, standing with veterans of both World War I and II but plagued by his own memories.

"The Ghost of Sandburg's Phizzog" is Blei's own paean to his native city, a "nocturne in a deserted landscape." "The Chair Trick" is a story that works on both physical and spiritual levels. "Stars" is a wonderful evocation of childhood, a story of both the highs and lows of a friendship amongst young boys who all too soon grow up and apart.

*Meditations on a Small Lake* is a sort of continuation of Blei's other Door County books. In the introduction, Blei reflects on the curious and ironic circumstance of his books actually contributing to the urbanization of Door County. Articles by Tim Cuprisin and George Vukelich reinforce this idea. "I even got a call from a guy putting up a condo who said, 'you know, I put a copy of your book in every condo!'" (p.22)

Blei returns with a series of brief prayers and recorded observations taken down in his walks. "In Praise of Country Darkness" is the best essay in the collection and Blei reprints a few of his letters to the editor to close the slim book.

### NORBERT BLEI: SELECTED READING

• *The Hour of the Sunshine Now,* 1978, Story Press, Chicago, 123 pp.

• *Door Way: The People in the Landscape,* 1981, Ellis Press, Peoria, IL, 230 pp.

• *Door to Door,* 1985, Ellis Press, Peoria, IL, 242 pp.

• *The Ghost of Sandburg's Phizzog,* 1986, Ellis Press, Peoria, IL, 196 pp.

• *Meditations on a Small Lake,* 1987, Ellis Press, Peoria, IL, 88 pp.

# JACQUELYN MITCHARD

It was a cold February night with a sifting of snow blowing through the streets. The dozen or so people who braved the cold to attend the monthly meeting of the Madison Area Free-Lance Editors and Writers organization (MAFEW, for short) sat slouched in their chairs drinking tepid coffee and awaiting the arrival of the guest speaker. At three minutes past seven o'clock, she breezed into the basement room of the Middleton Public Library. Her hair, long and curly, tousled by the wind, framed an oval face wreathed in an apologetic smile. The guest was Jacquelyn Mitchard, a columnist for the *Milwaukee Journal-Sentinel.*

For the next 90 minutes, Jacquelyn Mitchard regaled us with stories and anecdotes taken from her columns, with a tip here and there on writing columns and how to contact magazines and newspapers in hope of landing a regular column yourself. Mitchard, her large brown eyes constantly glowing beneath the fluorescent lights, also spoke about the novel she had recently completed and which had been accepted by a major New York publisher. She said she hoped that people would like it and buy a few copies.

Little did we know that one person already had a copy and liked it. That person was Oprah Winfrey, the television host, who was just starting a new feature called "Oprah's Book Club." Oprah Winfrey made Mitchard's first novel *The Deep End Of The Ocean* the first selection for her book club. Within a few short weeks of Mitchard's appearance before those dozen or so chilled souls at the Middleton Public Library, *The Deep End Of The Ocean* was at the top of the New York Times' best seller list and the movie rights had been bought by actress Michelle Pfeiffer. A new career had begun for Mitchard, a widow with three, soon to become five, children.

Jacquelyn Mitchard was born in Chicago. She graduated from Rockford College in 1973 with a degree in English. Her

**Jaqueline Mitchard. Photo courtesy of *Wisconsin State Journal/Capital Times* newsroom library.**

early post-college years were a struggle as she balanced teaching high school English and waiting tables at area restaurants. She began writing professionally in 1976 as a weekly newspaper reporter. Her health was complicated by a near-fatal bout with a tubular pregnancy, recounted in her first book, a memoir called *Mother Less Child* published in 1985.

Mitchard moved to Madison, where she worked as a journalist for the Madison *Capital Times* and began writing a series of columns that she called "The Rest Of Us." In 1984, she switched to the *Milwaukee Journal-Sentinel,* where her column quickly developed a wide readership and would later be nationally syndicated. Mitchard had also previously written two children's books based on the life of early 20th century peace activist Jane Addams. The turning point for Mitchard came when she went to a writer's camp for three weeks and began working on *The Deep End Of The Ocean*. The genesis of the book was a dream Mitchard had about a child disappearing in the midst of a crowd.

In *The Deep End Of The Ocean*, we see Beth Cappadora attending her high school's 15-year reunion with her children in tow: Kerry, Vincent, and Ben. Ben has just turned 3 and, while Beth is registering at the Chicago hotel where the reunion is being held, Ben wanders away from Vincent's care and is presumed lost. At the end of nine hours of nerve-wracking suspense, Beth gives way to panic and has to be sedated.

After several weeks of fruitless searching, Beth returns home to Madison, where her husband Pat and his father Angelo have a thriving Italian restaurant business. But Beth — like Alice Goodwin in Jane Hamilton's *A Map Of The World* — falls into a fugue state of depression and refuses to acknowledge her husband or the other children.

Hoping to capitalize on her sudden popularity, Mitchard and Viking Press quickly put together a voluminous selection of her prior columns, *The Rest Of Us: Dispatches From The Mother Ship*. These 79 short essays cover the gamut of topics, mostly parental in nature, but also there are essays on baseball, bonfires, cemeteries and Laura Ingalls Wilder. At times painfully human, at times wildly humorous similar to humor columnist Erma Bombeck, these essays offer lessons in life and living as well as death and dying. "A Star To Steer By" tells of her first husband's early death from cancer and her own nascent beginnings as a writer and the faith she had to rely on when everything else was crashing about her.

Mitchard's next novel was *The Most Wanted*, a tale told from the viewpoints of two vastly different women. The first is Arley Mowbray, a 14-year-old girl desperate for love, who at first corresponds with, and then meets and marries a much older man serving time in a Texas prison. The second voice is that of Annie Singer, a lawyer and public defendant who, despite the rigorous demeanor demanded by her profession, attaches herself to Arley's plight. *The Most Wanted*, like Mitchard's first novel, tends to drag in places and turns overly melodramatic in others, but does show a maturing of Mitchard's writing style.

*A Theory of Relativity* was Jacquelyn Mitchard's third novel, published in 2001. The story involves a cusstody battle over an orphaned 1-year-old girl named Keefer.

### JACQUELYN MITCHARD: SELECTED READING

- *The Deep End of the Ocean,* 1997, Viking Press, New York. 434 pp.
- *The Rest of Us: Dispatches from the Mother Ship,* 1997, Viking Press, New York. 255 pp.
- *The Most Wanted,* 1998, Viking Press, New York. 282 pp.
- *A Theory of Relativity*, 2001, Viking Press, New York. 368 pp.

# Index